MW01119895

SOOTHING THOSE
ACHES AND PAINS

Credits:

Art Director: Peter Bridgewater
Editorial Consultants: Maria Pal/Clark Robinson Ltd

Picture credits:

The author and publishers have made every effort to identify the
copyright owners of the photographs; they apologize for any
omissions and wish to thank the following:

Paul Forrester, 14–15, 57, 59, 75; David Gallant, 16, 17; John
Heseltine, 13; Sally Launder, 41; The Mansell Collection, 11;
Chris Thomson, 80, 81, 82, 83; TWA Getaway Club 60, 77; John
Watney, 29, 39; Trevor Wood, 59, 63; Zen NW3, 13.

fit for life

SOOTHING THOSE
ACHES AND PAINS

C A S E Y   E D W A R D S

Gallery Books
an imprint of W.H. Smith Publishers, Inc.
112 Madison Avenue, New York
New York 10016

A QUARTO BOOK

This edition published in 1990 by Gallery Books,
an imprint of W.H. Smith Publishers, Inc.,
112, Madison Avenue, New York, New York 10016

Gallery Books are available for bulk purchase for
sales promotions and premium use. For details write or
telephone the Manager of Special Sales, W.H. Smith
Publishers Inc., 112 Madison Avenue, New York, New
York 10016. (212) 532-6600.

ISBN 0-8317-3899-5

The information and recommendations contained in this book
are intended to complement, not substitute for, the advice of
your own physician. Before starting any medical treatment,
exercise program or diet, consult your physician. Information is
given without any guarantees on the part of the author and
publisher, and they cannot be held responsible for the contents
of this book.

▶ CONTENTS

TENSION HEADACHES

A common form of headache, one that affects many of us, is caused by the problems of day-to-day life. We all suffer from periods of anxiety over everything from our jobs to our marriages. Every little upsetting moment adds to the stress of living. Tension headaches are often a direct result of this kind of stress.

With all the factors that might cause stress, it should be no surprise that tension headaches are quite common. The odd fact about tension headaches is that they vary in intensity and duration from person to person and even episode to episode. The distinguishing factor is that the general pain from a tension headache results in dull, constant throbbing. Unlike a migraine, in which the pain is sharp and piercing, a tension headache usually feels more like a heavy weight sitting on the head. Other tension headache sufferers liken the pain to a feeling of having having a very tight band tied around the forehead.

Although the length and duration of tension headaches vary, they generally fall into different categories. Some sufferers say that the pain begins during the day and gets more intense toward evening. Since scientists suspect the headache stems from accumulated tension, and since tension builds during the day, the progression toward more pain in the evening is understandable.

Other tension headache sufferers say that they wake up with the pain, only to have it ease up as they begin their daily routine. The explanation for this may be that their daily routine takes their minds off whatever event, such as marital problems or mortgage payments, that is triggering the attack.

Another factor that may trigger tension headaches is overloading your senses. Continual loud noises, such as police sirens or the hum from your desk's fluorescent light, may also start a tension headache.

The problem with finding the cause of tension headaches is that all the possible upsetting factors have a cumulative effect. If only one thing caused the stress, it would be easy to identify. Unfortunately, most of us are bombarded with a series of stressful situations every day. Only by learning how to cope with the stress can you hope to alleviate the pain of tension headaches.

Rushing for *work first thing in the morning can be sufficient to trigger off a tension headache.*

STRESS AND TENSION

Stress-related tension *can cause:*

Headaches

Eyestrain

Stiffness in the neck

Shoulder and chest pain

TREATING TENSION HEADACHES

Since most doctors attribute tension headaches to stress, the best way to treat them is to learn how to cope and relax. In today's world stress and anxiety are constant irritations. Any discussion about treating this kind of headache must deal with prevention.

In theory, the best way to prevent tension headaches is to isolate yourself from the world. Since this is impossible, it is best to learn how to ignore or cope with life's nagging anxieties. The world is not going to end because you've missed a train. Relax. There are enough external stress factors over which you have no control. Those that you can control, such as your temper, have to be dealt with so as to reduce the stress.

You can control certain external factors such as bright lighting in your office or even a loudly ticking clock. You cannot control, for the most part, the neighbor's crying baby or those screaming police sirens. You simply have to try to put certain external stress factors out of your mind to prevent the onset of a tension headache. For example, try playing soothing music around your house when the baby starts next door.

If you've been unsuccessful in preventing the tension headache, you then have to find a way to treat it. Try finding the right exercises to help you relax. If the attack comes on while you are work, try closing your eyes for a minute while you gently rub your temples. Many tension headache sufferers have found that playing soft music on their portable stereo headphones helps to ease the pain.

If the tension headache attacks you at home, try taking a warm bath or applying a heating pad to the back of the neck. Since the headache may be the result of fatigue or hunger try lying down to rest or having a light snack such as a piece of fruit. Even if you cannot fall asleep, just being in bed, perhaps reading a good book, can help you relax and ease the pain. Another possible treatment is the application of a cold washcloth on your closed eyes or forehead. Whatever the treatment, the aim is always to relax your stressed system.

If the pain continues, your doctor may want to give you an examination to rule out any underlying physical problems. At that time, he or she may prescribe a pain-killing medication.

Learning how to cope with everyday sources of stress – simply getting to work during the rush hour above, for example – is a first step toward minimizing tension headaches.

Stress-related tension can cause headaches, eyestrain, stiffness in the neck, shoulder pain and chest pain.

HANGOVER HEADACHES

Nobody likes to suffer from a hangover. Combined with the nausea, fatigue and general feeling of illness is the throbbing pain of the hangover headache.

According to scientists, the hangover headache results only indirectly from the alcohol. The direct cause of the headache is fatigue. The alcohol may make you feel ill and nauseous, but lack of sleep leads to the headache.

Of course, alcohol does play some role in causing the headache. Alcohol affects the part of the brain that regulates metabolism and chemical interactions. As the alcohol level of the blood rises, the water content decreases, causing not only the dry mouth and thirstiness of a hangover but also the headache. Scientific studies show that alcohol causes the brain's blood vessels to expand. These enlarged blood vessels cause the throbbing pressure common during the hangover headache.

One way to prevent the hangover headache is, of course, not to drink. If you must drink, try to have drinks diluted with water or fruit juice. The more alcohol you drink, the more likely you are to have a hangover.

Many drinkers feel that different types of alcohol have varying effects on the hangover headache. This turns out to be true, according to recent medical studies. Certain drinks, such as Scotch, rum and brandy, have elements that tend to stay in the body's system longer than drinks such as vodka and gin. Logically, the longer these elements remain in the system, the longer is the recovery period from a night on the town.

Another factor contributing to the hangover headache is your mental state prior to drinking. When a person drinks to get rid of anxiety or stress, he or she is more likely to suffer a hangover. Although it hasn't been proven, the theory is that the brain's recovery power is weakened by the stressful situation that brought about the urge for a few drinks.

Most home remedies to cure hangover headaches are based more on fiction than fact. However, there may be some scientific basis to the adage that drinking lots of water before going to bed prevents a hangover. Remember, alcohol upsets the water content of the blood. Replenishing the water might lead to fewer enlarged blood vessels in the brain, which would reduce the hangover headache. Drinking more alcohol definitely does not help. Aspirin can help relieve the headache, but the only thing that really helps is time.

Absinthe became the most popular
French café drink by the 1890s and
had such a pernicious effect that it was
eventually banned altogether. Detail
from The Absinthe Drinker by
Degas.

11

MSG HEADACHES

The MSG headache, also called Chinese Restaurant Syndrome strikes the victim as a throbbing pain that usually appears right above the eyes. In some victims, the pain is accompanied with a swollen sensation in the head. The headache is caused by a commonly used food additive, monosodium glutamate (MSG). A salt of a natural amino acid, MSG is used in some prepared foods to enrich the flavor; it is commonly used in Chinese cooking, which is the reason for the alternative name.

Today many Chinese restaurants allow their patrons to order dishes without MSG, but keep in mind that MSG is used in many non-Chinese restaurants as well. If you are a frequent sufferer of the MSG headache, just tell your waiter to make sure it's left out of your food!

Besides the headache, the MSG syndrome can produce a tightness in the chest and a numb feeling in the neck and arms. Although the headache can be very painful, it usually subsides after a few hours. The MSG headache usually begins about 30 minutes after the meal. Some studies have shown that MSG in very small doses is safe. However, since it's impossible to determine your threshold dosage without a laboratory examination, you're better off omitting MSG entirely.

Of all the dishes served in Chinese restaurants, the soups, such as won ton or egg drop, usually contain the greatest amount of MSG. If your favorite Chinese restaurant doesn't allow you the option of selecting "MSG-less" food, then you can probably minimize the ill-effects by skipping the soup.

Recently a series of medical studies has shown that large quantities of MSG can lead to more serious side effects than just the Chinese Restaurant Syndrome. In laboratory rats, MSG destroyed the brain cells that control such factors as appetite and body temperature. Since these tests, most baby-food manufacturers have voluntarily removed MSG as an ingredient.

Since the Chinese restaurant headache naturally subsides in a few hours, there's no need to panic if you get one. One of the best things to do is relax. Don't apply any additional stress, such as a long drive at night, or looking at a glaring television screen, to your system. Let the MSG naturally pass through your system. Many people recommend drinking water once the headache begins. Water, however, may lead to a further bloating sensation and if so this remedy should be avoided.

...BLE D... ...ISH AND LI... ...AFOOD OUST THE C... ...ES AND BATTER ENCRUS... ...ERHAPS ENCOUNTERED IN THE ... ...VEGETARIANS ARE WELL PROVIDED F... THE HEALTH AND HEADACHE CONSCIOUS APPRECIATE THAT ZEN W3 IS A MONOSODIU... GLUTAMATE FREE ZONE.

*ome **Chinese restaurants** now dvertise vegetarian and MSG-free ecialties.*

13

HOT DOG HEADACHES

Many people suffer from headaches after eating bacon, hot dogs, ham, and other processed meats. These processed or cured meat all contain a form of nitrite, a chemical used as a preservative. Unfortunately for the consumer, in addition to causing headaches, nitrates are a potential cancer-causing agent.

The headache associated with nitrites usually comes on about 2 minutes after eating the processed meat. The throbbing pain seems to center at the front of the head just above the eyes. Besides the headache, the victim commonly has a reddened face. This red face and the throbbing headache are because the nitrites open (dilate) the blood vessels in the brain and head.

One way to prevent the hot dog headache is to stop eating nitrite-containing products. Processors use the chemical to give meats longer shelf-life and to make them appear redder. In today's health-conscious society, some producers offer nitrite-free bacon and hot dogs.

If you decide to buy the special nitrite-free meats, you'll have to prepare your system for a shock. Although the meats will taste like normal hot dogs, salami, and so on, they will appear almost brown in color. Without the nitrites, there is no artificial redness to the meat. In addition, if you buy nitrite-free meats, you should use them quickly, since they lack preservative. However, what you miss in color or shelf-life, you'll make up for in a healthy diet!

Unfortunately, there is little that can be done once you have a hot dog headache. Since the sharp, throbbing pain in your forehead is chemically induced, you must let it run its course before the headache will subside. Generally speaking, the pain will go away in a few hours. You should rest as much as possible, keeping your pulse to a minimum. Since you are feeling the throbs with each heartbeat, it makes sense to keep that rate down. At times this may be a little difficult, since so many hot dogs are eaten at events such as ballgames or carnivals, where loud noises and bright lights seem to aggravate the headache. If you are in that situation, try to find a quiet place, even a restroom, and get away from the noise. The less your body has to react to external, stressful influences, the easier it'll be to cope with the hot dog headache.

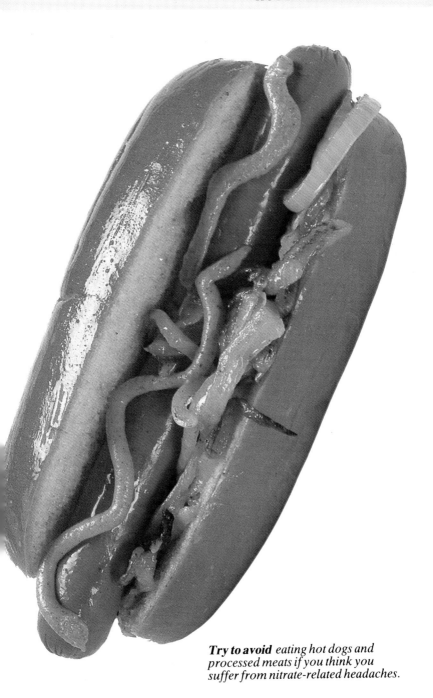

Try to avoid *eating hot dogs and processed meats if you think you suffer from nitrate-related headaches.*

FROZEN FOOD HEADACHES

A pain doesn't have to be from a serious illness to be annoying and discomforting. We can get a severe headache just from eating ice cream or drinking cold soda. Sometimes referred to as the "ice cream headache," this pain comes soon after the quick consumption of an especially cold food. The headache's pain is centered either in the middle of the forehead or on one side of the face. Another symptom of this headache is watering of the eye, which may be accompanied by a general swollen feeling on that side of the face.

Although very little in terms of scientific research deals with the frozen food headache, it is suspected that the headache is caused by some sensitive nerve endings in the mouth or throat. When the ice cream is eaten at a slow pace, the nerve endings have a chance to adjust to the frigid temperature. As more of the ice cream is eaten the nerve endings become "numbed" and there is no headache. However, when you gobble down the ice cream, preventing those

Be careful how you consume ice cream. Eat slowly to avoid the headaches caused by cold or frozen food.

ensitive nerves from adjusting to the sudden temperature drop, ney might go into a shock-like state. In many ways the situation is ke what happens when you pour an ice-cold liquid into a hot glass. he abrupt change in temperature often causes the glass to crack. If owever, you pour in just a little liquid and allow the glass to "cool own," the chances of it breaking are reduced. Essentially, this is hat goes on in your mouth and throat. When you eat only a little e cream at a time, the nerves become used to the temperature and ou do not get the headache.

Now that we have given you the reason for the headache the trick preventing one from starting. Simply put, you shouldn't just novel cold foods or liquids into your mouth. Eat them slowly, iving the nerves a chance to adjust. But if that chocolate chip ouble cone is just too irresistible, don't worry. If you feel your yes begin to water and that pain zaps your head, try drinking a lass of room-temperature water. The water will calm down the xcited nerves, bringing the mouth in general back toward the ody's normal temperature. This will make the headache disappear nd soon you can continue eating the ice cream before it melts.

SINUSITIS

Sinusitis is an inflammation of the membranes that line the fou sinus cavities within the bones of the face. The two forms that caus you the aches and pains are acute and chronic. Acute sinusit consists of short, sharp attacks, usually brought about by the sprea of germs into the sinuses. Chronic sinusitis usually develops if yo have some condition, such as an allergy, that tends to block one c more of the drainage holes from the sinuses to the nose. Howeve chronic sinusitis is relatively rare.

When you have a cold, the inflammation usually spreads int your sinuses. If your system is run down or a particularly virule germ is attacking you, one or more of your sinuses may becom acutely inflamed. If the sinus is completely blocked, you will e perience a throbbing pain and a general feeling of illness. Th classic symptoms of acute sinusitis are headaches and a heav aching feeling in the face which tends to get worse when you ber down. Your nose runs until the sinus gets so inflamed that draina is impossible. If the blockage occurs in the sinus above the ja your teeth may ache and you may mistakenly blame a "toothache for the pain. If you press the bone over an acutely infected sinus is quite painful.

In chronic sinusitis there is little tenderness. Without the tende ness it is possible to tolerate the runny nose and mild, dull hea aches. Colds in your head are worse than normal, however, an tend to last longer. Chronic sinusitis frequently brings on attacks sore throat, laryngitis, or bronchitis.

If you are suffering from a form of sinusitis, go to your docto For acute sinusitis, your doctor will probably recommend that yc rest indoors, keeping your head upright if possible. Nasal deco gestant drops or spray will probably be prescribed to reduce th swelling in the sinus. Another method to relieve the pain is inhalir the steam from a kettle very carefully — it's hot! Breathing steam helps to drain the sinuses. If your condition is severe, th doctor will probably prescribe a suitable antibiotic.

Although over-the-counter and prescription nose drops may gi relief in cases of acute sinusitis, it is best to not make a habit using them. Their helpfulness decreases with use and they m; make you feel worse in the long run. It has also been shown late that nose drop usage may actually be habit-forming.

In cases of acute sinusitis where the sinus remains blocked, th doctor sometimes must puncture the sinus and wash it out.

THE SINUSES

Pain around the eye and a swollen lid may indicate infection of the frontal sinus

Toothache is a symptom of an infected maxillary sinus

Discharge from the nose lessens as sinus becomes blocked

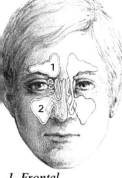

1 *Frontal sinuses*
2 *Maxillary sinuses*

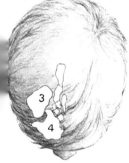

3 *Sphenoidal sinuses*
4 *Ethmoidal sinuses*

Mucus draining down throat can cause further infection

The four sinuses, *hollow cavities within the bones at the front of the skull, may become inflamed through the spread of infection when you have a heavy cold.*

HEADACHES AND SERIOUS ILLNESS

A headache may, in rare circumstances, be a symptom of a serious illness. Since it is not recommended that you run to the hospital every time one develops, you should be on guard for other symptoms. If the headache comes on quickly and you then feel weakening or paralysis of a limb, or a loss of consciousness or vision, seek medical attention at once. A headache with one of these complications may stem from a more serious illness such as brain tumor, stroke, or temporal arteritis (a chronic inflammation of the arteries of the brain).

If the headache is associated with a brain tumor, the pain will usually be in a fixed area of the head and may feel worse if you cough or reach down. Unlike migraines, which have periods of no pain, the brain tumor headaches are constant, building in pain during the day. The tumor headache may also be accompanied by loss of feeling in a limb and fatigue. If you are suffering from this type of pain, see your doctor at once. Many tumors can be successfully treated if discovered early.

Many people who have suffered a stroke say that they first felt a severe headache, accompanied by sensory loss and fatigue.

In people over 55, especially women, the headache may be a sign of temporal arteritis, a disease of the arteries in the head. The first pain is a throbbing in the temples or on one side of the head. Any movement that draws on the facial muscles proves painful. For this reason, sufferers from temporal arteritis may have trouble chewing their food. Look for red, tender blothes on the temples. If you think you might have temperal arteritis, see your doctor. In many cases it can be treated with drugs; if untreated, it could lead to stroke.

The brain is a very complicated part of your body. Any pain in the head area may be caused by a variety of factors. Look for signs other than the actual headache if you suspect a more serious illness. If in doubt, see your doctor. Many times just the knowledge that a routine physical shows nothing is enough to relieve the pain, while worrying needlessly over a potential serious illness may lead to more headaches!

The circle of Willis is made up of the arteries that supply the brain with most of its blood. A blockage of one of these arteries is a leading cause of stroke, one of the first symptons of which is a severe headache.

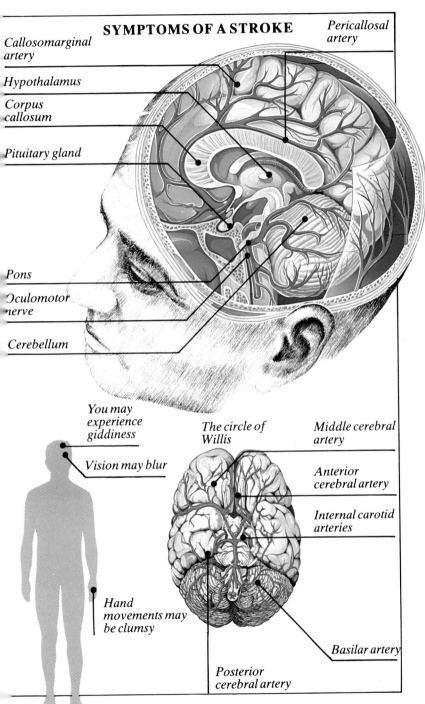

SYMPTOMS OF A STROKE

Callosomarginal artery

Hypothalamus

Corpus callosum

Pituitary gland

Pons

Oculomotor nerve

Cerebellum

Pericallosal artery

You may experience giddiness

Vision may blur

Hand movements may be clumsy

The circle of Willis

Middle cerebral artery

Anterior cerebral artery

Internal carotid arteries

Basilar artery

Posterior cerebral artery

21

MIGRAINE HEADACHES

Migraine is a common disorder likely to start after puberty an
disappear after the age of fifty. Women suffer from migraines mor
frequently than men, roughly in the ratio of seven to three. Th
most significant symptom is very severe headaches.

Migraine headaches usually cannot be traced to one specifi
cause. The head pain is undoubtedly due to a reaction in th
arteries of the scalp, eye sockets, face, and even the base of th
brain. At the height of the attack, the surface arteries may seem t
be swollen and generally feel tender to the touch.

Migraines can be triggered by a substance called tyramine, foun
in such foods as cheese, red wine, and chocolate. Sometimes sub
stances made by the body itself may be the cause.

SYMPTOMS

Before a migraine headache begins, there may be a slight bloatin
due to fluid retention. The effects on vision are like a shimmerin
heat haze; things may seem to appear moving in waves. The visio
may then get blurred and distorted.

Sometimes the migraine sufferer gets a numbness that usuall
affects one hand and spreads up the arm to the face, including th
mouth and tongue. Sometimes, speech may become slurred.

These early symptoms last about twenty minutes and are fo
lowed by the headache. The main characteristic of the headache
its severity. At its height, the sufferer may vomit and be unable t
bear bright lights. The headache may last for hours. Often th
passing of a large quantity of urine signals the end of a migrain
headache.

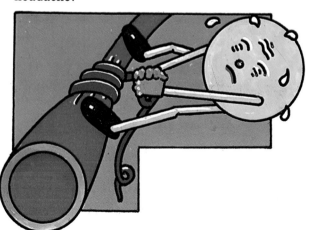

*Oxygen
deprivation in
parts of the
brain, caused b
dilation of the
arteries,
produces the
major symptom
of migraine –
often described
as a feeling that
the nerves of the
head are being
squeezed (left).*

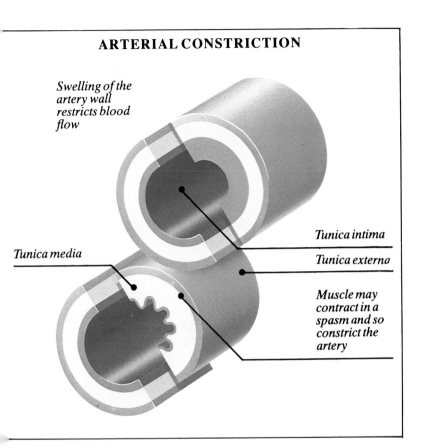

ARTERIAL CONSTRICTION

Swelling of the artery wall restricts blood flow

Tunica media

Tunica intima

Tunica externa

Muscle may contract in a spasm and so constrict the artery

DIAGNOSIS

Simply put, migraine symptoms are the result of a swelling of the arteries that supply the brain. This swelling prevents certain parts of the brain from receiving oxygen and other necessities. This explains why you may experience numbness in a limb prior to the actual headache. The arteries to the part of the brain controlling your limbs are preventing the sensations in your arm or leg from being delivered, leading to the tingling feeling that often precedes the migraine headache.

There is usually no problem in recognizing the migraine. Your doctor will take your medical history, asking if any family members suffer from migraines. If you are a woman, your doctor will ask if you are taking an oral contraceptive pill, since these sometimes trigger migraines. If you are over forty, the doctor will take your blood pressure and probably test your cholesterol level and thyroid function.

Treatment

It is generally not necessary for your doctor to perform elaborate tests to diagnose migraine. If you are a frequent migraine sufferer you should know a few self-treatment procedures. When you begin to get the blurred vision or numb limb that precedes your headache, you should prepare for it. Try to find a quiet place and if possible lie down. If the attack begins while you are a work, try closing your office door and sitting comfortably. If you share an office, excuse yourself and seek a quiet refuge, such as the rest room. Since some of the symptoms might include nausea the bath room might be a good place to be anyway!

If the nausea persists and becomes a problem in your day-to-day life, see your doctor. He or she may prescribe an anti-nausea medication. Take the medicine at the first sign of the migraine symptom for the maximum effect.

Blurred vision *can indicate the onset of severe migraine. Find the quietest place that you can and try to relax.*

Dairy products, *citrus fruits, red wine and chocolate are all known to cause migraines. Eliminate them systematically from your diet until you identify the specific food that brings on your headaches.*

Another scientific finding is that a mild prescription sedative can help to relieve the pain from migraines. If you begin to suffer an attack, and your doctor has given you a sedative, take it. Tests have also shown that the more sleep you get, the better the odds are that you'll have less pain. For this reason, it is probably a good idea for migraine sufferers to keep away from coffee and caffeine. Since both coffee or any other caffeine source, such as most colas, increase the heart's pumping activity, the logical choice is to do without. The more the heart pumps, the stronger the blood flow will be through those stressed arteries in the brain.

Another factor is how quickly you treat the migraine. The longer you wait to treat an attack, the more difficult it can be to control. It seems that the body's defense system reacts strongly to the migraine causes. The longer the cause goes untreated, the more the body focuses on the problem and therefore the longer are the pain-related symptoms.

Once the headache begins you must try to relax your system. Keep as still as possible, think calming thoughts, and soon you'll be through the most painful part of the migraine headache.

If it is impossible *for you to avoid traffic jams or other migraine-inducing situations, try light meditation, or simply altering your daily routines.*

PREVENTION

The best way to treat a migraine headache is to prevent its occurrence. It is possible that your migraine is associated with some routine factor in your life. Stress, diet, and even your sleep patterns can affect migraine headaches.

Certain food substances have been shown to induce migraines. Some people suffer from migraines caused by chocolate, cheese, citrus fruits, fried foods, and even red wine. To determine what foods may be causing your migraines, you have to use a little trial and error. Try eliminating one of the above from your diet and see if the headaches persist. Sometimes just a slight change in your eating habits rids you of the migraine.

Stress is another big migraine factor. Most of us can remember a major emotional event that caused a bad headache. Since stress is mostly unavoidable in our daily lives, you have to find ways of coping with it instead. Some people try medication. Simply learn to think about some calming, serene scene, such as a beach. When you are in a stressful situation, such as a traffic jam, light meditation can help get your mind off the trouble.

Massage is another way to relieve stress. The manipulation of those tense back muscles and shoulders is a physical way to ease the stress. Not only does the massage physically make you think of something other than the stress that may have contributed to the migraine, but the revived circulation caused by the rubbing tends to reduce the throbbing headache.

Since even a simple headache may lead to stress, you should try to prevent those too. Scientists have found that lack of sleep and disrupted sleep patterns lead to headaches. The body's normal routine is thrown off, resulting in a migraine.

Other factors that should be avoided if you frequently suffer from migraines are bright lights, loud noises, and too much exercise. All of these tend to trigger migraines, since they cause the body to respond in an abnormal way. Again, if you feel a migraine coming on in a crowded, bright place, seek a quiet area and try to relax.

If you find it is impossible to get away from one of these trigger factors because your life is too stressful, you might consider altering your lifestyle. Migraines are no way to spend your life. Take the time to evaluate how you live and see if there are ways to make some changes. For example, if you continually are in stress-causing traffic jams on your way to work, consider taking a train or a bus — will give you time to read a good book, while you let the driver worry about the bumper-to-bumper crawl!

CLUSTER HEADACHES

If you've ever had what seems like a series of bad headaches you may suffer from cluster headaches. These severe headaches can last anywhere from a week to a few months. There are frequently a few lapses in the pain, but the recurrence of the headache brings back the agony of the illness and depression.

Cluster headaches are a unique form of migraine because they affect men four times as often as women. Our theory is that the hormonal swings present in women somehow help to prevent the cluster headache.

Besides the pain in the head, the cluster headache brings with it discomfort around one eye. The eye may begin to water and eventually turn red. Sometimes the fluid backs up near the sinus cavities leading to blockage and an eventual sinus headache.

Cluster headaches may begin at any time of the day or night. Unlike migraines, the cluster headache isn't preceded by any warning sign, such as tingling in the hand or blurred vision. The cluster just begins with a series of mild headaches. If you are a sufferer you soon begin to realize that a few of these mild headaches may build and last for months.

Like many other kinds of pain, cluster headaches can be triggered by alcohol. The alcohol causes the original headache and that has a "snowball" effect with the cluster syndrome. People who suffer from cluster headaches are advised to keep away from alcohol.

The good news about cluster headaches is that they occur in only five percent of serious headache cases. There are a variety of drugs that your doctor might prescribe to try to reduce the pain.

In addition to drug therapy, some doctors recommend that cluster headache sufferers try acupuncture, massage, and even biofeedback. In biofeedback training, you are taught to alter the blood flow to your hands and head. Learning this technique is time consuming but may help reduce the pain.

Another simpler way to ease the pain is to relax in a quiet room with a cold compress gently placed over the eyes and forehead. The more you soothe the body, the less you may suffer!

The Chinese medical system called acupuncture has identified more than 300 points along the body (right) that, when stimulated, seem to alleviate a number of conditions, including cluster headaches. Acupuncture needles are very fine and round-ended, so blood vessels are no broken.

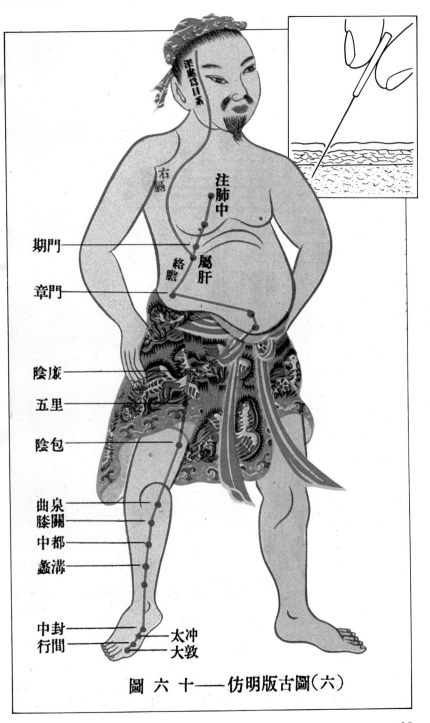

期門
章門
陰廉
五里
陰包
曲泉
膝關
中都
蠡溝
中封
行間

注肺中
屬肝
絡膽
右脅

連膈喉目系

太冲
大敦

圖 六 十——仿明版古圖(六)

EYESTRAIN

Another common cause of headaches is eyestrain. In our daily lives, the eyes play a major role. If you have an uncorrected vision problem, you may suffer from some type of eyestrain. In addition, bright lights, smog, and soot can all contribute to eyestrain.

If you suffer from headaches whenever you read too much or drive long distances, you should see a doctor or optician. The headaches might be caused by straining your eyes to see properly. The complicated arrangement of the different parts of the eye enables a sharp image to be focused on the retina. To put things simply, if the image is not correctly focused on the retina, your eye strains to make the adjustment. If you have trouble seeing objects at a distance, you have myopia or short-sightedness. In this condition, the lens of your eye focuses distant objects someplace in front of the retina. In hypermetropia or far-sightedness, near objects are focused behind the retina. If you are far-sighted, you might develop a headache from reading close print, like books or magazines. In either case, eyeglasses will help the lens to focus properly on the retina and end the eyestrain.

In today's society another common cause of eyestrain is smoke. Since heavy doses of industrial smoke may be hard to avoid, at least you can try to cope with the cigar and cigarette smokers of your world. When possible, sit in the nonsmoking section of your train or restaurant. While at work, politely ask the smokers around you to keep the puffing to a minimum.

Glare from bright lights or sunshine can also cause eyestrain. This can be avoided by making sure the light is soft and even when you are working or reading; try to have it come from behind or above you. Wear sunglasses when outdoors in bright sunshine, especially at the beach or when on snow (when skiing, for example).

Looking at a computer screen for long periods of time can also cause eyestrain. The screen will be easier to see if you avoid fluorescent lights. Look up from your work every ten to fifteen minutes and give your eyes a short break.

EYES AND VISION

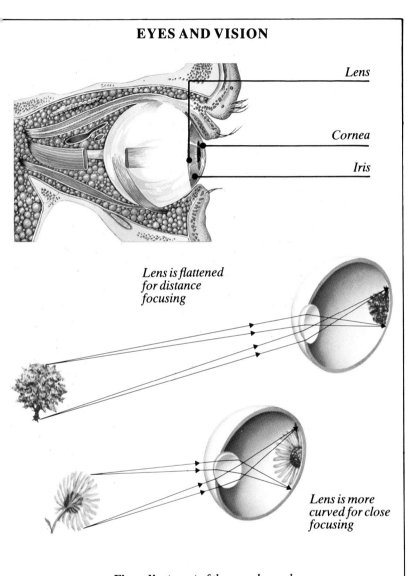

Lens

Cornea

Iris

Lens is flattened
for distance
focusing

Lens is more
curved for close
focusing

Fine adjustment of the muscles and
ligaments surrounding the lens
enables us to focus our eyes. Distant
vision requires the lens to be pulled
into a disc shape; in close vision the
lens becomes more circular. If either
of these mechanisms is faulty
eyestrain results unless the deficiency
is corrected by the proper eyeglasses.

CONJUNCTIVITIS

Conjunctivitis is a very common inflammation of the membrane covering the majority of the eyeball and lining the eyelids (the conjunctiva). The disease is quite common among children, largely because of their tendency to rub their eyes when they are tired even though their hands are dirty. This can lead to the virus infection known as "pink eye".

Conjunctivitis can be due to a virus or bacteria; it is highly contagious in this form. It may also be caused by an allergic reaction irritants such as pollen or cosmetics. Conjunctivitis is slightly more common in areas of high pollution.

When the membrane is inflamed, the eyes are red and watery with the redness stretching toward the cornea. Sometimes there is discharge around the eyelids. The lids may be swollen, while the eye feels as though there is grit under the lids. If both eyes are affected, the infection is probably bacterial; a viral infection usually affects just one eye.

Conjunctivitis is easy to diagnose. In mild cases, the problem responds to routine home treatment such as eye washes, ointment or drops. If only one eye is infected, it is obviously important to prevent the infection from spreading to the other eye. This is best done by observing the rules of simple hygiene and using disposable tissues and towels. If you are using drops, take care not to infect one eye with material from the other. You should also avoid touching your face and wiping it with towels that may be used by other people.

Cold compresses and dark glasses are comforting. If the problem continues, your doctor should be consulted. If the conjunctivities is caused by bacteria, he or she may prescribe antibiotic drops or ointment. If the problem is an allergic reaction, an antihistamine may be prescribed.

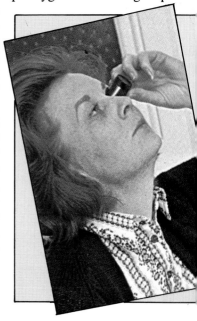

An eye bath can help to ease the symptoms of conjunctivitis.

INFLAMMATION OF THE CONJUNCTIVA

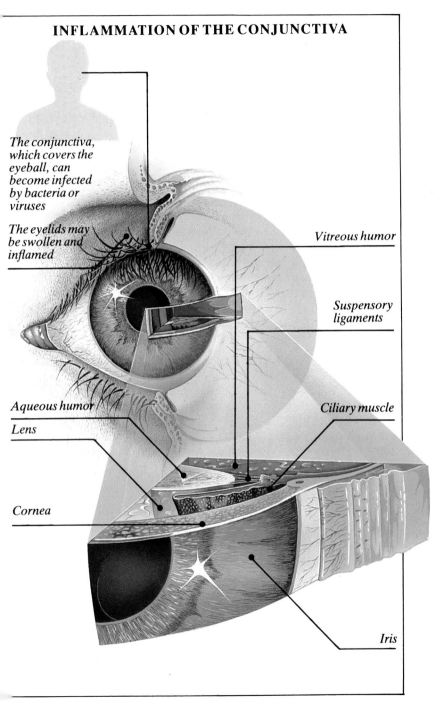

The conjunctiva, which covers the eyeball, can become infected by bacteria or viruses

The eyelids may be swollen and inflamed

Vitreous humor

Suspensory ligaments

Aqueous humor

Lens

Ciliary muscle

Cornea

Iris

EARACHES

Infections of the ear, whether of the outer or middle ear, frequently cause pain. Middle-ear infections are usually more severe and are often accompanied by loss of appetite, fever, and a general feeling of illness.

The Eustachian tube, which leads from the back of the throat (the pharynx) to the middle ear, may become inflamed and blocked off, causing a severe earache. This may be associated with a throat infection, as germs pass along the tube from the throat.

Earache may also be a symptom of dental decay, teething in a young child, or a boil in the ear canal. Sinusitis, particularly infections of the area behind the ear, may also cause an earache.

Earaches stemming from the outer ear are commonly caused by a wax build-up. The wax normally functions to protect the outer ear's fine layer of hair. It helps prevent bacteria and dirt from entering the ear canal and middle ear. The wax also keeps the eardrum lightly lubricated. However, if a piece of wax is touching the ear drum or blocking the ear passage, hearing obviously suffers.

If hardened wax needs to be removed, you should consult your doctor. In some cases, the doctor may arrange to have your ear syringed or drained. If your doctor prescribes eardrops, it is important not to damage the inner part of your ear when using them. Tilt your head to one side. Gently squeeze the drops into the center of the outer ear. Fold over the exterior portion of the ear (the pinna), and allow the drops to run inside naturally.

If you have an earache, you can initially treat it by placing a warm hot-water bottle, wrapped in a towel, under the affected ear while in bed. Aspirin may also give relief. It is important not to push cotton balls down the ear canal, as the delicate, inflamed tissues and eardrum may be accidentally damaged. A serious earache that is not relieved by mild heat should be seen by a doctor.

An earache that stems from the outer ear may be caused by a build up of hardened wax that requires syringing or the application of drops. More commonly, earache originates in an infection of the Eustachian tube, which connects the middle ear to the back of the throat (opposite, top).

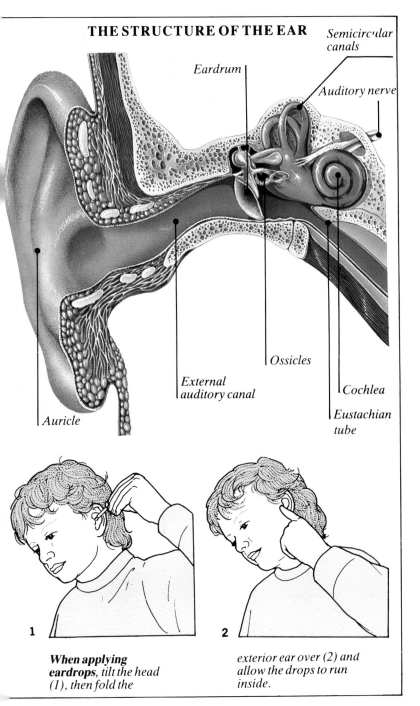

THE STRUCTURE OF THE EAR

Semicircular canals

Eardrum

Auditory nerve

Ossicles

External auditory canal

Cochlea

Eustachian tube

Auricle

When applying eardrops, *tilt the head (1), then fold the* exterior ear over (2) and allow the drops to run inside.

1

2

LARYNGITIS

Laryngitis occurs when the mucous membrane of the voice bo
(larynx), including the vocal cords, become inflamed. It is usuall
acute, that is, a short, sharp infection that often develops in th
course of a cold.

Attacks of acute laryngitis can also be precipitated by excessiv
shouting, singing, or speech-making, particularly if you are no
trained in voice projection. If you are subject to bouts of sinusitis
you are very likely to get laryngitis. Several attacks of acute laryn
gitis may lead to a chronic state, where your voice is never clear an
gradually changes to a lower pitch.

The inflammation that is the chief cause of laryngitis may sprea
down from the nose and throat when you have a common cold, sor
throat, influenza or such infections as measles. The inflamed laryn
looks red and swollen, while the vocal cords, which normally loo
bright and lustrous, look dull and pink.

You may be slightly feverish with acute laryngitis. You will have
dry, tickling discomfort in the neck, together with a dry cough tha
produces saliva. The main problem is hoarseness. On waking, talk
ing is uncomfortable and your voice sounds hoarse. The feelin
increases as you use your voice until it nearly vanishes.

An attack of laryngitis rarely lasts more than a few days, and
very rarely serious. Keep warm and stay indoors, as one of th
main irritants of the larynx c cold air. The coldness and dryness c
the throat can be partly relieved by the warmed moisture of inhale
steam. This remedy may also help to clear the nasal passages fro
the common cold. It is advisable to put as little strain on the voc
cords as possible, so keep your talking to a minimum. Treatmen
that may ease the discomfort without actually curing the illne
include traditional cough mixtures, honey and lemon drinks an
additions to the steam inhalation such as menthol or peppermin

Vocal cords that have a dullish hue, rather than their normal bright color, are among the symptoms of laryngitis that a laryngologist will take into account to confirm his diagnosis.

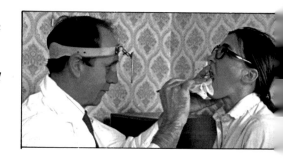

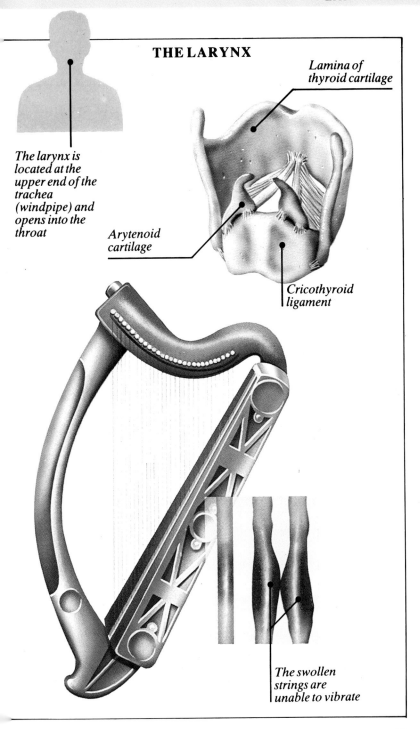

THE LARYNX

Lamina of thyroid cartilage

The larynx is located at the upper end of the trachea (windpipe) and opens into the throat

Arytenoid cartilage

Cricothyroid ligament

The swollen strings are unable to vibrate

HAY FEVER

Hay fever is a form of allergy. In it, the membrane lining the nose is sensitive to one or more kinds of pollen and, as a result, swells and becomes inflamed. It is an extremely common ailment, affecting between five and ten percent of the population of the United States. Although pollen is the best known and most widespread cause of this allergy, which is also called allergic rhinitis, other fine airborne particles such as house dust and animals such as horses or cats can also cause a reaction.

Doctors say that hay fever has a typical allergen-antibody reaction. Hay fever sufferers carry an antibody in the lining of the nose, bronchial tubes, eyes, and skin. When the pollen, as an antigen, comes into contact with the antibody, a reaction takes place on the surface of the cell and various substances, including histamine, are released. As a result, the surrounding cells swell as they become filled with fluid and there is a watery discharge, with

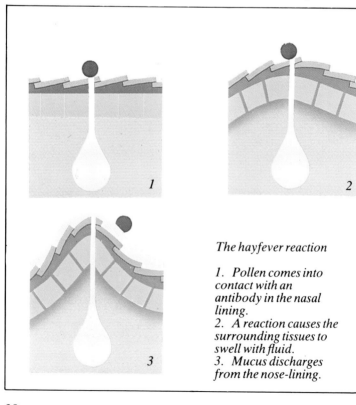

The hayfever reaction

1. Pollen comes into contact with an antibody in the nasal lining.
2. A reaction causes the surrounding tissues to swell with fluid.
3. Mucus discharges from the nose-lining.

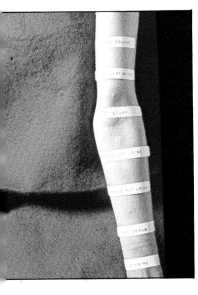

Sensitivity tests *are sometimes conducted to isolate individual allergies. The skin is exposed to several suspected irritants and the various reactions recorded. Once the allergen has been determined the allergy can be treated with a course of injections.*

an outpouring of mucus. In other words, the body reacts as though dealing with a powerful infection, rather than harmless grains of pollen.

When the pollen season arrives, you'll sneeze almost constantly. Usually your nose runs like a faucet, though at times it is congested and blocked. Your eyes are red and sore because pollen grains have irritated the transparent layer over the eyes. There is normally a significant amount of pollen in the air only during the summer months. During these months there will be somewhere between 0 and 400 pollen grains per cubic meter of air. At 50 grains per cubic meter, anyone who is going to have a hay fever attack starts sneezing.

Your doctor will probably use sensitivity testing to determine your type of allergy. If you are found to have a specific allergy, you could have a series of desensitizing injections over a period of weeks. Usually, this must be repeated annually for three years, and does not give complete relief. You should avoid walking in fields of grass or ragweed. Antihistamine drugs, both prescription and over-the-counter, may reduce the symptoms, but they can make you sleepy, especially if combined with alcohol, and you should not drive while taking them. Decongestant sprays will make your nose more comfortable. However, decongestant sprays tend to damage the delicate mucous membranes if they are taken regularly; you may also develop a tolerance to them; a consequence of this is that they can actually make the situation worse.

TOOTHACHE

Most toothaches are caused by decay of the enamel and dentin (the hard substance surrounding the pulp) of the teeth. Dental decay (caries) is a particular hazard to people who eat candy or sugary foods, to people who do not clean their teeth regularly or efficiently, and to many children.

Dental decay results from the presence of plaque on the teeth. The plaque contains bacteria and residual carbohydrates from food. The bacteria attack the carbohydrates, which as a result form acid. This acid eats away at the enamel of the tooth, causing a cavity and opening the interior pulpy area to infection, which causes inflammation and pain.

A tooth with a developing cavity may become sensitive to cold, heat, and sweet substances. As the cavity enlarges, this sensitivity becomes more and more acute until the dentin is eaten away, the nerve becomes irritated, and the toothache begins. An abscess may form at the root of the tooth.

You must see a dentist as quickly as possible to treat a toothache. In the meantime, there are a few steps to take to relieve the pain. Sometimes aspirin or an over-the-counter painkiller takes away the

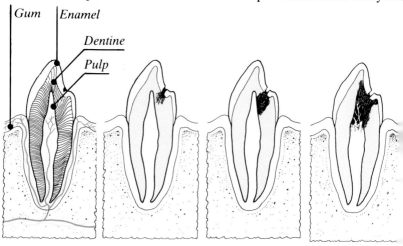

Gum *Enamel*

Dentine

Pulp

Bacteria *act on the sugar in food to produce acid, which eats into tooth enamel.*

Erosion *creates a cavity that may extend to the underlying dentine.*

If the decay *is not halted, bacteria have a chance to infect the pulp.*

Inflammation *of the pulp puts pressure on the nerve and causes toothache.*

initial pain. Some doctors recommend the application of an icepack to the area. The ice tends to numb the area, making it less sensitive. You should never apply heat to the tooth or gums if infected. Since heat tends to enlarge the blood vessels, you may actually be spreading the infection to other areas of the mouth. If the toothache is caused by the loss of a filling, you can apply a little oil of cloves to a piece of cotton and then pack the cotton into the hole. If you've lost a filling, you must get to your dentist as soon as possible. An exposed nerve or hole in the tooth is an open invitation for more infections!

BRUSHING YOUR TEETH

Prevention is the best treatment for toothaches. Brush your teeth with a fluoridated toothpaste; floss them regularly. Avoid sugary snacks and eat a balanced diet. And see your dentist every six months for a professional cleaning and a checkup.

Clean upper teeth *by brushing downward. Lower teeth should be brushed with an upward action.*

Tilt the toothbrush *at an angle to brush the backs of upper and lower teeth.*

Brush *the grinding edge of the teeth using a rotating movement to get into crevices.*

Finish *with dental floss to remove any remaining food debris between the teeth.*

STIFF NECK

One of the more annoying of minor aches and pains comes from stiff neck. It doesn't matter what kind of condition you're in — t neck and upper shoulders have a lot of muscles that must do a lot work. These muscles support and move the head, which usua weighs between fifteen and twenty pounds. Although used eve day, the neck muscles are most often ignored during exerci Anybody can build up the biceps and triceps, but how many of work on the neck?

What usually causes a stiff neck is an abnormal movement of t head or shoulders that stretches the neck in an abrupt way. F example, a common cause of stiff necks is whiplash from an aut mobile accident. When your car is hit, particularly from the re your body is thrown violently forward and then back. Since t head is relatively unsupported, it whips forward and back. T result is often a serious stiff neck or even fractured vertebra Wearing a seatbelt will not prevent whiplash, but it can keep it fro being as serious.

Of course, many of us have suffered stiff necks from oth causes. Any abnormal stretching, whether it's from a vigoro toweling of the hair or a quick glance, can lead to a stiff neck. Y can even get a stiff neck from sleeping in a bad position. T sternomastoid muscle runs down either side of the neck and acts incline the head toward either shoulder. Sometimes in your slee you stretch that muscle at an awkward angle and wake up unable move your head.

If you have suffered a stiff neck as the result of an accident, y should see a doctor. X rays may be taken to see if you have fracture. In other instances, you can treat the neck with war compresses, hot baths, heating pads and massage. The idea is relax the neck and shoulder muscles until they regain their resi ency.

Relax neck muscles by tipping your head back, to the right, forward and to the left in a slow and gentle rolling motion.

THE SITE OF A STIFF NECK

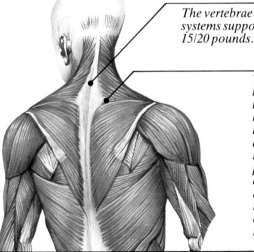

The first two cervical vertebrae of the neck form a pivot joint, allowing the head to move up and down, and from side to side. Tensed or damaged muscles will restrict this movement.

The sternomastoid muscle runs down the side of the neck and allows head movement from side to side. A common site for neck pain, even stretching too vigorously can cause this muscle to stiffen.

The vertebrae and associated muscle systems support a head weight of 15/20 pounds.

The trapezius muscle covers the shoulder blade, holding it in position and allowing it to rotate. Long periods spent crouched over a desk, or basic bad posture can cause tension in this muscle.

43

STOMACH ACHES

Stomach ache is a general term often used to describe various form of indigestion. When we eat something, our digestive system breaks down the food in a series of chemical processes. Given the complexity of it all, it's small wonder that we occasionally have indigestion.

OVEREATING

When you eat too much at once, the stomach cannot digest the food fast enough. The excess food causes a feeling of fullness, and the excess stomach acids that then develop cause a stomach ache. The best cure is avoidance!

HEARTBURN

A severe burning sensation behind the breastbone is generall known as heartburn. The most common form of heartburn i caused by gas that builds up in the stomach and presses the stomach against the diaphragm (the domed sheet of muscle separating the chest from the abdomen). This sort of heartburn is easily treated with over-the-counter antacids and antigas medications. Spicy o fried foods often cause heartburn; avoidance is the best solution.

HIATUS HERNIA

Your gullet (esophagus) passes from the mouth to the stomach. I goes through the diaphragm in an opening called the hiatus. Some times the tissue around the hiatus weakens and allows the lowe portion of the esophagus to protrude through it up into the ches cavity. This is called a hiatus hernia, and it is very common. Mos people who have a hiatus hernia are never bothered by it. How ever, in many people it can cause severe heartburn because aci from the stomach is able to well up into the lower esophagus. Th pain can sometimes be so severe that it is mistaken for a hear attack.

The heartburn and pain of a hiatus hernia are often relieved b over-the-counter antacids. Since the problem occurs most often i obese people, try losing weight. Try not to bend over, especiall after a meal, and don't wear tight belts or clothing. If often helps t elevate the head of the bed. And smoking and drinking alcoho make the problem worse — another good reason to quit smokin and drink lightly.

If you have very severe chest pain, go to an emergency center. I

LOCATION OF A HIATUS HERNIA

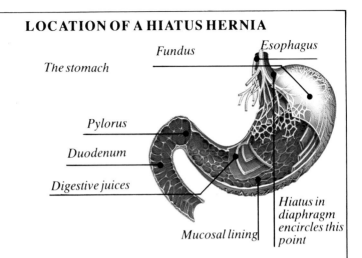

Fundus

Esophagus

The stomach

Pylorus

Duodenum

Digestive juices

Mucosal lining

Hiatus in diaphragm encircles this point

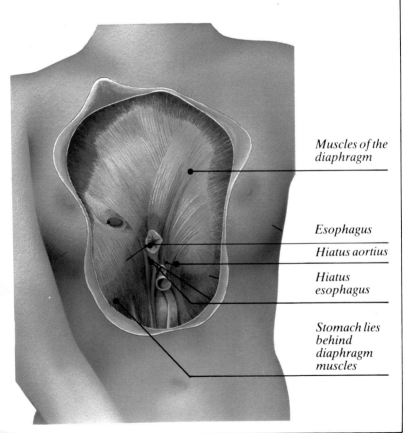

Muscles of the diaphragm

Esophagus

Hiatus aortius

Hiatus esophagus

Stomach lies behind diaphragm muscles

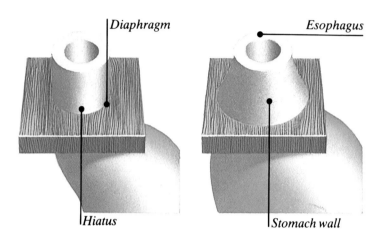

HOW A HIATUS HERNIA OCCURS

Diaphragm

Esophagus

Hiatus

Stomach wall

The simple diagram *above shows how part of the stomach forces its way through the hiatus in the diaphragm. Because the stomach's digestive juices can sometimes well up into the lower esophagus, heartburn may be a painful complication of the condition – it may even be severe enough to be confused with a heart attack.*

just might be a heart attack, and if it isn't the emergency personne can help ease the pain of a hiatus hernia.

MOTION SICKNESS

Even expert sailors can get seasick. If you suffer from motio sickness, there are some things you can do to relieve the symptom: Be careful about what you eat before starting a trip. Don't starv yourself. Eat easy-to-digest foods like fruits and carbohydrate: Avoid greasy or fatty foods, alcohol, and carbonated drinks. Drin plenty of fluids. Sit facing in the direction the vehicle is moving, an look straight ahead. Perhaps the best advice is to concentrate o something else aside from the state of your stomach — talk, sing, c admire the scenery. Over-the-counter medications to comba motion sickness are available. Many of these contain dimenhy drinate, an antihistamine and anti-emetic drug. Your doctor ca prescribe additional medication.

BACKACHES

The human body, miraculous as it is, isn't really very well designed for standing upright. All the stresses, strains, and pressures of moving on two legs end up on the back. Almost all of us will suffer from back pain at some point in our lives.

ACUTE BACK PAIN

Acute back pain may start suddenly, after heavy lifting or vigorous exercise. Chronic back pain develops slowly over a long period of time. Acute backache in a young, fit person is often caused by muscle or ligament strains. The problem usually disappears in a few weeks without treatment, but is helped by bed rest on a firm surface, pain-killing medicines, and muscle relaxants. Heat, from an infrared lamp, heating pad, or hot-water bottle wrapped in a towel and placed on the back can also help relieve the pain.

CHRONIC BACK PAIN

Chronic backache is an entirely different problem. It is usually associated with poor posture, often combined with stress. In women, the pain may become worse during pregnancy or before and during a period. Remedial exercises to improve the posture may relieve the symptoms of backache; relaxation techniques to reduce stress may also help.

One very common backache problem is lumbago, a severe, aching pain in the muscles of the lower back. It can be brought on by exposure to cold, damp conditions or by straining the muscles of the lumbar (lower) region of the back. It often begins with an abrupt spasm in the lower back while bending, standing up from a sitting position, or lifting something heavy.

SLIPPED DISK

Slipped disk is the common name for what happens when one of the disks of tissue that act as cushions between the vertebral bones of the spine slips out of position. A slipped disk can occur at any age. In younger people, the cause is usually a definite injury or strain. In the elderly, the backache is more likely due to a general degenerative condition.

The backbone consists of a curved, flexible column of 24 separate bones. Between each of the movable bones, or vertebrae, is a cushion of cartilage (disk) that allows for a small amount of movement and also acts as a shock absorber.

HOW A SLIPPED DISK OCCURS

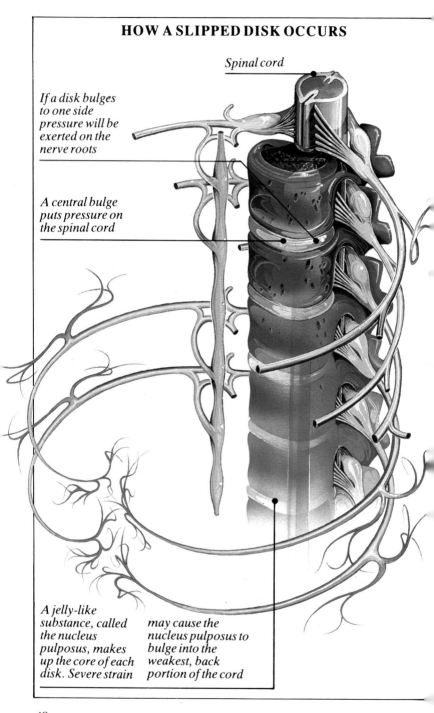

Spinal cord

If a disk bulges to one side pressure will be exerted on the nerve roots

A central bulge puts pressure on the spinal cord

A jelly-like substance, called the nucleus pulposus, makes up the core of each disk. Severe strain *may cause the nucleus pulposus to bulge into the weakest, back portion of the cord*

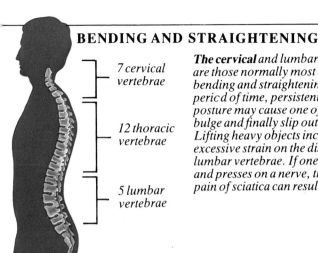

BENDING AND STRAIGHTENING

7 cervical vertebrae

12 thoracic vertebrae

5 lumbar vertebrae

The cervical and lumbar vertebrae are those normally most affected by bending and straightening up. Over a period of time, persistent faulty posture may cause one of the disks to bulge and finally slip out of position. Lifting heavy objects incorrectly puts excessive strain on the disks of the lumbar vertebrae. If one of these slips and presses on a nerve, the severe pain of sciatica can result.

If a lumbar (lower-back) disk slips out of place and presses on a nerve, the usual result is sciatica. The pain of sciatica is severe; it is usually felt on one side in the back, one side of the buttocks, and the back or side of the thigh and calf. If a neck disk is involved, you are likely to have severe pain, with tingling and numbness usually affecting the arm and hand on one side.

A doctor should be consulted at once if a slipped disk is suspected. An X ray must be taken to determine the location and extent of the problem. During the period of severe pain your doctor will probably recommend rest and painkillers. A cervical collar for the neck or a corset for the back may be useful during the recovery period. Special exercises will strengthen your back and neck muscles and provide a greater degree of flexibility. Avoid lifting anything heavy for the foreseeable future. If you suffer from chronic or recurrent sciatica, your doctor's advice may be to recommend surgery.

Since we now know how easy it is for a disk to slip out of place, proper posture, lifting, and exercise may prevent it from happening. The back can be strained by such ordinary activities as slaving over sink that is too low or even working with a stooped posture at your desk. The back should be kept straight at all times.

Slipped disks in the lumbar region are caused most often by heavy lifting. The heavy object need not be the washing machine; many a parent has slipped a disk by lifting a small child! The rule to remember when lifting is: always bend the knees. This takes some of the strain off the lower back.

TREATING BACK PAIN

Once you have suffered a backache, the treatment should be gradual enough to ease the pain without causing any further stress to the back. When the backache is healed, you must learn how to avoid a recurrence.

Acute backache, caused by a sudden strain to the back, is generally easy to treat, although it takes a few weeks to go away completely. Your doctor will probably recommend bed rest. If your mattress is soft, you should put a board under it to give you more support. The muscle strain has to have time to relax so that flexibility may return. For this reason, your doctor may prescribe pain-killers and muscle relaxants. Basically, these prevent you from feeling the ache and thereby keep you from tensing or flexing the injured area. Never combine these drugs with alcohol! If possible, you should apply heat to the damaged area. Warm baths are not recommended because the difficulty in getting in and out of the tub

*A **relaxing** holiday in the sun can help to accelerate recovery from a back strain*

ould further damage the back. Instead, apply a hot-water bottle or heating pad to the back area. If you have one, a heat lamp also aids the back. If you live in a warm, sunny climate, try lying in the sun, exposing your back to the warm rays.

Another form of treatment for backaches involves an assessment and alteration of your lifestyle. Obesity is a major cause of back pain, because the spine cannot support the extra strains that are put upon it. If you are overweight, you may be able to prevent or reduce back pain by going on a diet.

If you have a minor pain in the back, try gently stretching the affected area. Sometimes an easy stretch limbers up the muscles of the area, taking away the pain. If the pain is in your lower back, for example, lie down on your back with a pillow tucked under your flexed knees. Gently breathe in and hold it for a few seconds; then slowly exhale. What you are doing is a slight stretch of the lower back combined with a subtle relaxation of your entire body.

TAKING CARE OF YOUR BACK

Sleeping *on a firm mattress that supports the back and keeps the spine straight (right) can help to prevent or alleviate back problems. A soft mattress that sags in the middle is likely to distort your spine.*

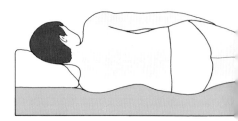

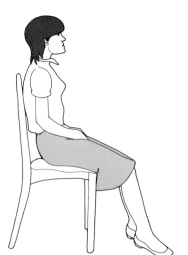

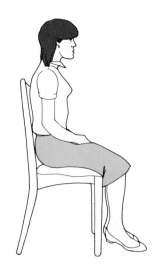

Sitting *in a slouched fashion (left) makes your back carry the*

strain of your body. To distribute the weight more evenly, sit erect in

THE SITE OF LUMBAGO

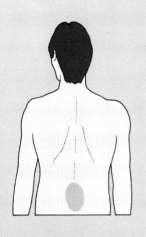

Muscle strain or *exposure to cold, damp conditions can bring on lumbago – an aching pain in the lower back (left).*

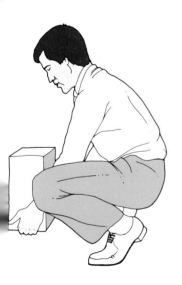

a chair with a back high enough to provide support. Lift objects

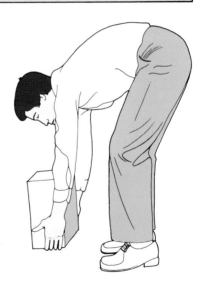

from a squatting position rather than bending your back.

PREVENTING BACK PAIN

Since most acute back pain is caused by a sudden strain to the back the logical thing to do is learn how to use your back properly. The back is an essential element in almost any movement of the body In fact, if you try to make most movements or lifts without using your back, you'll probably just injure another part of the body such as your arms and legs.

We lift things every day. Remember, it doesn't have to be a heavy object to cause back pain. Sometimes just bending down the wrong way can cause you to pull out your back. When the object to be lifted is on the floor, do not lift it by keeping your legs straight and bending your back. Instead, get down into a squatting position, keeping your back straight, and then lift the object by standing up as you straighten your legs.

PROPER POSTURE

Another cause of backaches is incorrect posture. How you walk sit, even sleep can affect the vertebrae of the back. Many of us develop bad posture habits as children and carry them into our adult life.

Sitting in a chair seems like such an ordinary event that few of us pay any attention to our posture. But look around you and you'll see people sitting in all kinds of positions. Slumped down, one leg draped over the arm of the chair, crossed legs — all these positions may lead to a backache because of the stress they place on the vertebrae.

When sitting in a chair, try to keep your spine as straight as possible. Make sure your chair has a back that is high enough to support you when you sit erect. Don't sit in a slumped or slouched position that puts the strain of your body weight on your back. By allowing your weight to transfer naturally down to the chair, no strain is put on your back. At first you must remember to check your posture. Once you have controlled the tendency to slouch, sitting properly in a chair becomes easy and natural.

While sitting, try not to cross your legs, since this places a strain on one side of your back. The top leg pulls on the back, perhaps putting it out of alignment. Since most of us habitually seem to cross one particular leg over the other, the strain affects only one side.

When going to sleep you must position yourself properly to keep your back from straining. First of all, use a mattress hard enough to support your back. A mattress that curves and bows in the middle is likely to distort your spine. Don't fall to sleep with your legs

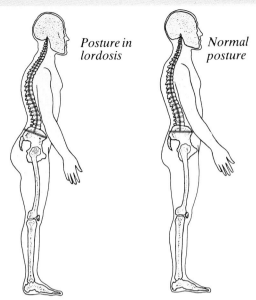

Lordosis is characterized by a forward tilt of the pelvis, and curvature of the spine, leading to an unnatural "S"-shaped posture. It can be caused by muscular weakness or bad posture, which can be corrected.

Posture in lordosis

Normal posture

crossed. Besides being bad for circulation, your back will be unnecessarily strained.

You can even throw your back out by walking incorrectly. As you take your stride, try to keep your spine upright. Too many of us walk hunched over, contributing to curvature of the spine that results in backache. Walk upright, with your shoulders back. Use your swinging arms to aid the movement; this reduces the strain on your lower back and legs.

Sleeping on a too-soft mattress may injure your back. Many of us wake up with backache, never really knowing the cause. A mattress that is too soft allows the spine to curve out of alignment, putting a strain on the vertebrae. If you can't afford a new mattress go to a lumber yard and get some lumber for your lumbar! A stiff board under your mattress will prevent the lumbar area of your lower back from slipping during the night.

Another good way to prevent backache is by strengthening those other muscles of the body that support the back. In particular, you should strengthen the stomach and hip muscles. In most movements involving the back, the hip and stomach muscles play a major role.

Any attempt to prevent backache must include a method to ease the tension and stress in your life. Tension causes the body to react by tightening the muscles. If a muscle doesn't get enough relaxation, it remains tight and flexed, inhibiting its function. A tightened muscle loses its ability to stretch, leading to stiff necks, backaches, and even headaches.

EXERCISES FOR THE BACK

There are many exercises that can help to prevent backache. Most of these concentrate on stretching and strengthening the muscles in the back, stomach, hips and buttocks. These muscle groups, if properly toned, can take much of the strain off the back.

Head Wobble

Since the spine stretches from the lower back all the way to the head, it's important to keep all the vertebrae locations limber. The head wobble keeps the neck and shoulder muscles stretched. Sit in a chair with both feet on the floor. Relax your arms by placing them at your sides. With your neck relaxed, gently roll your head around, beginning by reaching your chin toward your chest, then your left shoulder, up toward the ceiling, then your right shoulder, and back to the chest.

Abdomen Crunch

The stomach muscles are very important for supporting the back movements. Unfortunately, most people exercise the stomach incorrectly, resulting in more, not less, lower back pain! A good stomach exercise places the tension on the abdomen, not the back. Lie on the floor, slowly bend your knees up, and place your feet on the floor so that your heels are five or six inches away from your buttocks. Then reach out with both arms and grasp one knee. Tighten your stomach muscles and slowly pull the knee halfway to your chest, inhaling as you go. Release the knee to the original bent position as you exhale. Repeat with the other knee. Repeat five times with each knee.

Hip Flex

The hip muscles must also be developed to take some of the strain off the back. Lie on your back, and bend your knees until your feet are flat on the ground. Rest your arms by your sides with palms to the ground. Keeping feet and shoulders to the floor, lift hips a few inches and hold for a count of 5. Return to your starting position and repeat 10 times.

Back Relax

Lie on your back and look up at the ceiling. After any sort of exercise, you must cool down and relax the muscles. Roll your knees up to your chest and grasp them with both arms. Gently pull your knees in and breathe deeply. Hold it for ten seconds and

release. Repeat. What you are
doing is stretching and relaxing
those back muscles that you have
"worked out" during your other
exercises.

Head Wobble

Abdomen Crunch

Hip Flex

Back Relax

57

MUSCLE CRAMPS

A cramp is a prolonged and painful spasm of a muscle. Cramps are caused by many things: unaccustomed exercise, prolonged exercise, or sitting or lying too long in an uncomfortable position.

When you are suffering from the ache of a muscle cramp, there are a few things you can do.

● Stretch the affected muscle as much as possible by straightening it. If the cramp is in the back of the calf, for example, place one hand on the heel and the other on the toes. Pull the toes as far back toward the front of the leg as possible. Then flex the toes outward. Repeat.

● Once the muscle has started to relax, the ache starts to disappear. Use both your hands and massage the cramped area. If the cramp is in a place you cannot reach, get someone to help. By massaging the area, you increase the circulation of body fluids, helping to end the cramp.

● Like massage, a warm compress increases the flow of the blood to the cramped muscle. Use a heating pad or wrap a hot-water bottle in a towel and apply it to the cramp.

One way to reduce the likelihood of exercise-related muscle cramps is to cool down the system after working out. Too many people just jump into hot showers without letting their muscles relax. A good rule of thumb is to cool your system down for the same amount of time you warmed up before exercising.

NIGHT CRAMPS

Cramps in the legs that occur while sleeping are common, especially for older people. Although these may be a symptom of a more serious problem, night cramps are generally nothing to worry about. A glass of milk before bedtime may help prevent them; some people are helped by eating a banana. Raising the foot of the bed can also help.

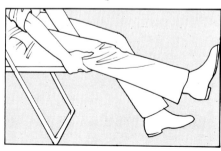

Ease calf muscle cramp by straightening and stretching the leg, flexing the foot back towards the body (left)

Cramp is *often caused by overworking muscles unaccustomed to exercise (right)*

MUSCLE STRAINS

A strain is an injury to a muscle in which the fibers are stretched or torn. Otherwise known as a "pulled muscle," the problem is a common sports injury. The tear usually results when the muscle is stretched beyond its limits; for example, when your arm is suddenly pulled too far backward or when you make a sudden movement that the muscles of your back are not prepared for.

If you are aching from a muscle strain you should take these steps:

● Make sure that you are not suffering from another injury, such as a broken bone which may initially seem to have similar symptoms. Frequently a person treats only a strain when the underlying injury is more severe.

● Do not attempt to "cure" or "work out" the ache by exercising

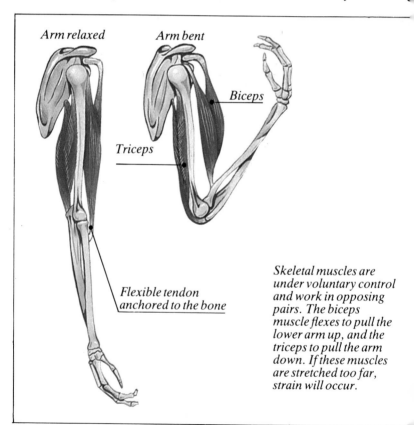

Arm relaxed

Arm bent

Biceps

Triceps

Flexible tendon
anchored to the bone

Skeletal muscles are under voluntary control and work in opposing pairs. The biceps muscle flexes to pull the lower arm up, and the triceps to pull the arm down. If these muscles are stretched too far, strain will occur.

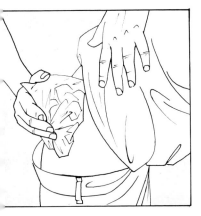 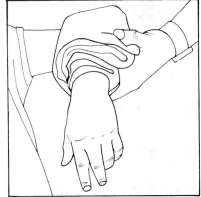

Immediate first aid for muscle strain involves applying a cold compress – such as an ice-filled bag – to the injured area. Follow this a little while later with heat treatment (a hot towel or bath).

the injured area. The best advice is to rest the affected muscles immediately.

● Gently massage the injured muscle. This will relieve the immediate pain.

● As soon as possible after the injury, apply ice to the affected area. (The ice should be wrapped in a protective layer of cloth or towels so as to not damage the skin surface.) The ice will reduce the swelling and numb the injured muscle, and usually lessens the pain considerably.

● Wrap an elastic bandage firmly around the injured area to support it. Don't bandage too tightly, however, or you will cut off the circulation.

● Elevate the injured area if possible.

● Later you may wish to apply heat in the form of a heating pad, a hot-water bottle wrapped in a towel, or a hot bath to the injured area. After the initial shock to the injured muscle, it's a good idea to increase the circulation so that the body's natural healing mechanisms may function. Since heat increases the blood flow where applied, it should be utilized once the injured area has been immobilized.

● If you are in doubt about the seriousness of the injury, you should consult your doctor. Fractures are difficult to diagnose without an X ray.

Many instances of muscle strain can be reduced if you remember that lifting or pulling can tear a muscle. If you haven't exercised a particular muscle and then suddenly attempt to use it, you're asking for a strain.

JOINT SPRAINS

A joint sprain is the result of a tear or an over-stretching of the ligaments surrounding and supporting a joint. Ligaments are bands of strong connective tissue between the bones of a joint that strengthen it and limit its movements to those for which it was designed. You'll know you've got a sprain because the joint will be quite painful, unable to support any weight, and may start to swell. In time, the injured area may redden or even turn black and blue.

If you have a joint sprain you should take these steps:

● Try to get into a comfortable position. Raise the affected joint and support it with cushions or a pillow. If you're not at home, improvise. Use a rolled-up jacket or even a pair of sneakers to elevate the joint. Elevation reduces the circulation to the area and reduces the swelling.

● Remove any clothing covering the joint and apply some ice wrapped in a towel. The ice will help keep the swelling down.
● Wrap an elastic bandage around the joint, snugly but not tight enough to cut off the circulation. Using a bandage or even an improvised sling, keep the joint immobilized. The less movement, the quicker the recovery. In addition, it is possible that the joint might be fractured and any movement could cause further injury. If the joint begins to swell, loosen the bandages at intervals.
● Start exercising the joint gently, without putting any weight on it, after 24 hours or so. Keep the joint elevated as much as possible.
● Don't attempt to do more than you are capable of. Joint sprains can be serious and medical attention may be required. See your doctor if the pain is still bad after two or three days.

There is very little you can do to prevent a joint sprain. Unlike muscles, the ligaments cannot be strengthened with exercise. If you've sprained a joint once, the likelihood of it happening again increases, since ligament damage takes a long time to heal fully.

Make sure *that you are in good physical shape if you participate regularly in team games. Injuries often occur through lack of physical – and mental – preparation.*

ARTHRITIS

Almost all of us develop arthritis at some point in our lives. Arthritis is a painful inflammation of the joints. The disease has been around since the days of the cavemen. In fact, until recently, when the most complete Neanderthal skeleton was reexamined and traces of arthritis were found, it was thought that early man walked slouched over. In reality, Neanderthal man probably just suffered from arthritis.

The pain of arthritis is caused by the inflammation of the membrane that helps to lubricate the joints. Over a long period, inflammation "eats away" at the cartilage and ligaments, even lessening the tendons. As the arthritis gets worse, the muscles surrounding the joint lose their strength and flexibility because you tend not to use them.

It has now been shown that the more execise you get, the stronger your bones, ligaments, and muscles become and the less likely you are to suffer from arthritis. Fifteen minutes a day of walking, jogging, tennis, or aerobics seems to be enough to keep the chances of arthritis to a minimum. On the other hand, certain sports, such as football and weight training, may lead to arthritis because of the wear and tear they place on the muscles and joints.

Another factor to be considered is your weight. Overweight people are prone to arthritis because the added weight puts stress on muscles and joints. In a similar way, good posture helps to prevent arthritis by keeping the stresses of movement distributed equally over your body.

If you feel that you may have arthritis, see your doctor. Prompt medical assistance has been found to help halt the rapid spread of arthritis. Since your lack of mobility from one arthritic joint may put a strain on another joint, fast treatment becomes important.

In treating arthritis the main goal is to reduce the pain from the inflammation as well as to increase the mobility of the joint. Aspirin, anti-inflammatory drugs, heat, and exercise are all important parts of treating arthritis.

OSTEOARTHRITIS
Osteoarthritis is a degenerative disease affecting the joints. As a consequence it tends to strike the middle-aged and the elderly almost exclusively. Usually many joints are affected, including the end joints of the fingers. The joints become painful, stiff and swollen.

DEGENERATION OF THE JOINTS

Joints that receive a lot of wear and tear, such as those in the legs, are the most prone to osteoarthritis. As the disease progresses, the cartilage lining the joint becomes increasingly less elastic until it finally cracks and ulcerates, making movement stiff and painful. Flexibility is further hampered by the development of osteophytes, bony outgrowths around the affected joint.

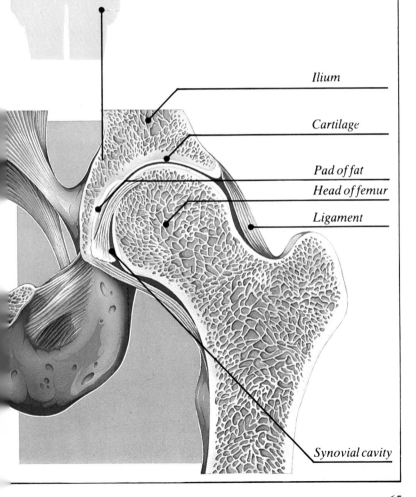

Ilium

Cartilage

Pad of fat

Head of femur

Ligament

Synovial cavity

As the body ages, the joints are more affected by wear and tear since worn tissue is not repaired and regenerated at the same rate as when you were younger. The effects of osteoarthritis are similar to what happens to leaves on a tree. When the leaves are young and flexible, they blow easily in the breeze while still attached to the stem. As the leaves get older, they become stiff and brittle, losing all flexibility.

In osteoarthritis the cartilage — the smooth, slightly elastic, sliding surface covering the ends of the bones in a joint—becomes soft. The parts subjected to the most wear such as the knees, hips, and fingers, are usually those most affected. The surface cracks, fragments, and ulcerates. At the same time, outgrowths of bone called osteophytes develop around the joint and may restrict its movement.

The first signs of osteoarthritis may be the development of hard bony swellings in the last joint of your fingers. They may be painful at first. Other joints, excluding the wrists, may be involved and become painful and stiff after use. Affected joints are generally limited in their range of mobility. They also creak or grate as they move; they may also be knotted and disfigured.

Once your doctor has diagnosed osteoarthritis, your treatment will involve several things. Excessive rest can be as bad as excessive exercise; both should be undertaken in moderation. Sensible measures include reducing your weight if necessary, especially the hip or knee joints are involved. Simple painkillers and anti-inflammatory drugs such as aspirin can be very helpful; your doctor may also prescribe stronger drugs to reduce the swelling and pain. Since pain in osteoarthritis seems to be influenced by the weather — cold and dampness increase pain and stiffness, for example - sufferers should dress warmly. Heat applications can also be soothing.

There is little evidence that so-called "miracle treatments" like bee stings or copper bracelets help arthritis. You will probably be better off following your doctor's advice.

RHEUMATOID ARTHRITIS

Rheumatoid arthritis is a long-term disease of unknown origin. can begin suddenly, affecting several joints and causing sudden pain and swelling or, gradually, affecting first one joint and then another. The disease affects women three times as often as men the peak age for its onset is between 25 and 55. Heredity also plays a part in its development; you stand four times the risk of developing rheumatoid arthritis is you have a close relative with the disease

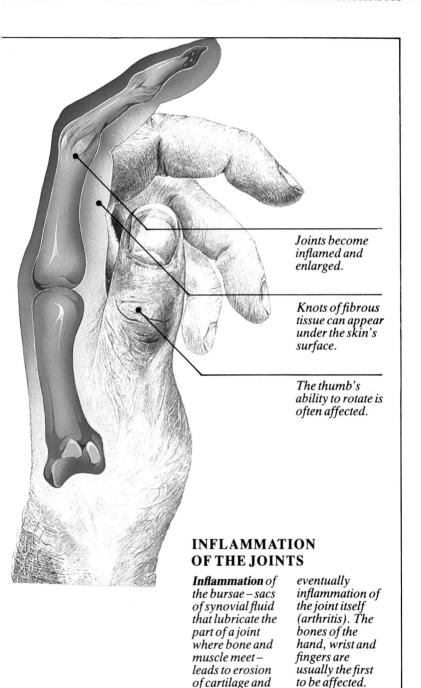

Joints become inflamed and enlarged.

Knots of fibrous tissue can appear under the skin's surface.

The thumb's ability to rotate is often affected.

INFLAMMATION OF THE JOINTS

Inflammation of the bursae – sacs of synovial fluid that lubricate the part of a joint where bone and muscle meet – leads to erosion of cartilage and eventually inflammation of the joint itself (arthritis). The bones of the hand, wrist and fingers are usually the first to be affected.

  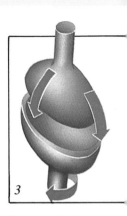

Freely movable joints, as they are known, are particularly painful if inflamed. They include

ball and socket joints (1), found in the hip and shoulder; ellipsoid joints (2), such as those

between the fingers and palm; and saddle joint (3), located in the ankles.

For some reason, the problem starts with overactivity in the body's immune processes. The effects of this show themselves in the membranes which form the lining to the joints, tendons, and bursae (the small cushions that protect and lubricate joints). When this lining gets inflamed, it grows thickly and roughly, eroding the cartilage that covers the bone end in a joint and even the bone itself. The process is painful, and the end result may be severe deformity.

The disease usually progresses gradually, with joints on both sides of the body affected symmetrically. Swelling in the joints of the hand and wrists is usually the first symptom to be noticed. If the disease is active, you'll have stiffness and pain in your joints when you wake in the morning, lasting for more than half an hour. Your sleep may be disturbed by pain and you may generally feel below average.

Other parts of the body can be involved. Your nerves may be affected, causing a pins-and-needles sensation in the legs and feet.

Your doctor will probably take X rays to diagnose the disease. Swelling of the soft tissues is visible to the naked eye, but the characteristic erosion of the bones near the joints will show up only on X rays.

Because the basic cause of the disorder is unknown, treatment cannot aim at more than control and modify its effects. Rest, keeping warm, and regular, gentle exercise are vital. Painkillers and anti-inflammatory drugs prescribed by your doctor will give you some relief. Almost half of all those who suffer attacks of rheumatoid arthritis recover completely.

RHEUMATOID ARTHRITIS

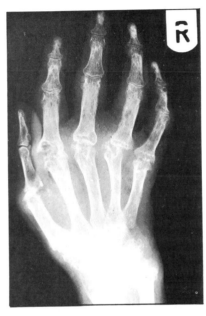

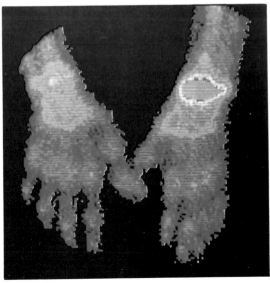

In general, rheumatoid arthritis first affects the hand and wrist joints then, in progression, those of the feet, ankles, knees and hips (above). The X ray (top, right) shows fingers that have become deformed over many years of the disease. Red areas on the thermogram (right) indicate where inflammation is most severe.

BURSITIS

Bursitis is an inflammation of the bursae, the small, fluid-filled pouches that act as shock absorbers in a joint and reduce friction between the bones, muscles, and ligaments. In response to an injury, an infection, or, most commonly, to unusual pressure, the membrane lining the pouch increases its production of fluid. As a result the bursa swells up, restricting the movement of the joint and causing pain and tenderness.

Bursitis may develop in any of the large joints of the body, such as the shoulder, the ankle and the elbow. Often it is associated with the presence of a bunion at the joint between the big toe and the foot. Another common form of bursitis, however, occurs around the patella, or kneecap. This condition, known as housemaid's knee, can be caused by constant kneeling. It develops in people who constantly apply pressure to or bang their knees. People who scrub floors, lay carpeting, or work on loading docks are liable to develop "housemaid's knee." Since the patella is so rigid, the bursa between it and the skin gets a lot of abuse. The more the bursa gets bumped, pressed, or injured, the greater the likelihood of bursitis developing.

The treatment for bursitis is fairly simple. Stay off the joint as much as possible, and the condition will probably go away in a week or two. In severe cases, the excess fluid must be drained by

Infection, injury or – more usually – continued pressure to a joint may result in the characteristic tenderness and swelling of bursitis. In this condition, the bursae become inflamed, producing more fluid than usual and restricting movement.

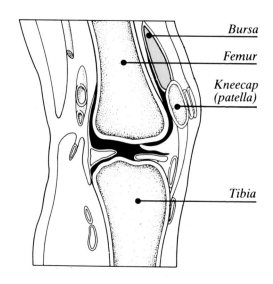

Bursa

Femur

Kneecap (patella)

Tibia

our doctor. A syringe draws out the excess fluid and the joint is bandaged tightly until the pain and tenderness disappear. In some cases, antibiotics may be given to prevent any infection. Bursitis is also treated with anti-inflammatory medication and occasional cortisone injections.

To prevent bursitis, you can buy special kneepads that provide an extra layer of protection to the bursae. Obviously, the more you put between your knee and a hard surface, the less wear and tear on your bursa and kneecap. If bursitis keeps recurring in any joint, it may be necessary to remove the affected bursa. Nowadays this is a fairly simply procedure.

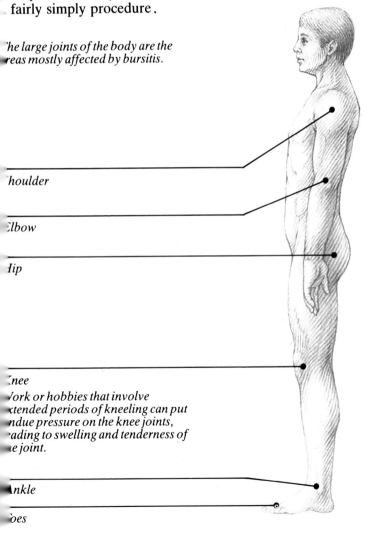

The large joints of the body are the areas mostly affected by bursitis.

Shoulder

Elbow

Hip

Knee

Work or hobbies that involve extended periods of kneeling can put undue pressure on the knee joints, leading to swelling and tenderness of the joint.

Ankle

Toes

TENDINITIS

Tendons are fibrous tissues that attach muscles to bones. Some tendons are surrounded by sheaths of tissue that contain synovia fluid to lubricate the tendon and reduce friction.

When a tendon is damaged, overstretched, or infected, a condition called tendinitis develops. The area affected becomes sore and even more painful if moved. Tendinitis is common in the shoulders and heels, but one of the most common forms is called tennis elbow.

Tennis elbow is a painful condition thought to involve inflammation of the tendons of the muscles directly related to the movement of the tennis racket. The tendons of the forearm at the point where they join the one of the upper arm gets quite inflamed. As a result of the inflammation, the elbow becomes sore. When the arm is rotated and the wrist moved, the condition gets even more painful. Since these are the movements associated with various racket sports, the condition has been branded tennis elbow.

Tendinitis can strike anyone, even those who have never picked up a tennis racket. Any motion that damages the tendons may lead to this painful inflammation. People who get the disorder in the shoulders, elbows, or wrists generally use their arms and wrists an abnormal amount, at work or at play. Golfers and bowlers, for example, often develop tendinitis.

Since the condition may develop from too much stress on the tendons, you may try to prevent tendinitis by wearing a special elastic brace. This brace, which slips over the elbow or the wrist provides added support without restricting movement of the limb. Acting like an exterior set of tendons, the elastic brace takes the tension and pressure off the body's natural tendons.

Tendinitis usually clears up with rest after a few days. Aspirin can help relieve the pain. In most cases, as long as no further strain is put on the tendon, the condition goes away.

In cases where tendinitis doesn't clear up or where the inflammation is very painful, your doctor may treat it with injections of a steroid drug.

Tennis elbow, although not always directly related to sport, can be caused by racket games that require almost continuous use of the elbow.

SHIN SPLINTS

Shin splints are a condition that arises when abnormal stress is put on the tendons and muscles in the front of your calf. These muscles and tendons are responsible for lifting the foot. When shin splints develop, the muscles of the shin pull away from the leg bones, leading to inflammation and pain in the lower leg surrounding the calf. Since these muscles and tendons primarily act as shock absorbers for your leg and foot, any inflammation is very painful.

There are many causes of shin splints, but they most common occurs when you repeatedly plant your feet on hard surfaces, especially at the wrong angle or when the legs aren't warmed up. This is why, for example, people who play basketball on hard wooden floors or runners who work out on concrete suffer the aches of shin splints.

One of the first signs of shin splints is a tightening sensation in the lower leg. After any type of exercise, you have a tight feeling that will not go away even after periods of rest.

To prevent shin splints, keep your body fit. Don't exercise unless you are warmed up. Don't exercise on hard surfaces, and make sure you wear workout shoes with enough cushioning to absorb the pounding. Shoes with cushions work as exterior shock absorbers to aid the body's natural mechanisms.

To fight the pain and reduce the inflammation of shin splints you can:

● Apply ice immediately after the symptoms first develop.

● With mild shin splints you can still exercise, if you do it gently and on soft surfaces. If you work out at home, try buying a pad to absorb the shocks of all those jumping jacks.

● If the pain is too severe, stop exercising for a few days.

● Wear cushioned shoes to ease the stress on your tendons and muscles.

● If possible, try swimming or bicycling to keep in shape until the pain subsides. Swimming and bicycling are excellent exercises that keep the pressure off the legs and feet.

Jogging is an excellent exercise, but to avoid shin splints take care to wear shoes with a cushioned insole and refrain from running on hard surfaces for any length of time, until you are used to it.

FOOT PAINS

Since we all have to walk to get anywhere, the last thing you want is foot pain. Unfortunately, the foot is a very sensitive part of the body — and it constantly takes the brunt of your body's weight.

BUNIONS
One foot problem that commonly develops is bunions. A bunion is an inflamed, bony protrusion that sticks out of the side of the foot from the joint of the big toe. The cause of the problem is often shoes that are too pointy or tight, causing the big toe to turn inward and forcing the joint outward. A pharmacist can supply you with shields and lifts that protect the bunion. If bursitis or arthritis develops in the bunion, surgery may be necessary.

INGROWN TOENAILS
Another common foot pain comes from ingrown toenails. The condition arises when the tissue surrounding the nail pushes against a nail that has been trimmed too closely. If there is no sign of infection, press a small piece of cotton under the painful nail, forcing it to grow out of the flesh. If the toe has become infected, see your doctor. You can prevent ingrown toenails by cutting your nail straight across.

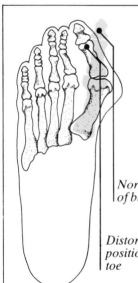

Normal position of big toe

Distorted position of big toe

BUNIONS

Inflammation of tissue, *most often through badly-fitting shoes, can lead to a bunion that distorts the shape of the big toe.*

INGROWN TOENAILS

A toenail *that has been cut too closely may become ingrown if tissue around the nail pushes against it.*

CORNS

A frequent cause of foot aches is corns. These are thick layers of dead skin cells that form on the tops of the toes. They are caused by poorly fitting shoes. The pressure of the shoes against the corns can cause tenderness in the tissue beneath the corn. To treat corns, wear shoes that fit properly. Soften your feet with an ointment such as petroleum jelly, and the corns will eventually disappear. Cushioned adhesive rings that fit around the corn and protect it are available from your pharmacy.

CALLUSES

Calluses develop from friction, usually on the heel or ball of the foot. Here the problem is probably caused by loose-fitting shoes that allow the heel of the foot to rub against the base of the shoe. Wearing high heels can cause calluses on the balls of the feet. To remove calluses, rub the area with a pumice stone and then wash with a cream-based soap for added moisture.

To prevent most of these foot pains, you should take care to get properly fitting shoes. Your shoes should be neither too tight nor too loose and yet supply you with just enough support. A good rule of thumb is to try both shoes on before buying. Even though it says it's your size, remember that every company has size templates that are slightly different. Try it on and if the shoe fits . . . buy it!

CORNS

Habitually wearing shoes that are too tight causes thick layers of dead skin cells – corns – to form at pressure points on the tops of the toes.

CALLUSES

The heel and ball of the foot are susceptible to calluses, areas of hardened, thickened skin, if subject to constant friction.

PREMENSTRUAL SYNDROME

Premenstrual syndrome (PMS) is a condition involving emotional and physical changes that affects many women up to ten days before a menstrual period. More than half of all women experience some PMS symptoms, which often worsen after the age of 35.

Although the symptoms vary with the woman, they may include irritability, weight gain, depression, insomnia, tenderness of the breasts, headaches, and a bloated stomach. Another symptom is quick emotional swings from elation to depression and back again

Fluid retention usually occurs before a period, which may account for some of the symptoms, but PMS seems to be mainly due to hormonal changes prior to menstruation. To help adjust to the premenstrual time, you should eat a high-protein diet that is low in water-retention substances such as salt and carbohydrates. In some cases diuretics such as caffeine may be taken to reduce the water build-up. In severe cases, treatment with the hormone progestin, before a period, may be prescribed. Vitamin B$_6$ therapy with pyridoxine is helpful in some cases, while painkillers may be given for the headaches. Some women may be given mild tranquilizers to relieve the anxiety during the worst days.

Since there is no real way to avoid PMS, the best you can do is ease the symptoms. If you are a PMS sufferer it might be advisable to maintain a diary to keep a record of when the symptoms occur. Sometimes just knowing when you're about to enter your PMS cycle will help relieve the tension. You will know when to begin modifying your diet. Also, if you can alert yourself and your family to the onset of the syndrome, you might have an easier time coping with the wide emotional swings.

The menstrual cycle is determined by hormones, levels of which are regulated by the hypothalamus in the brain. It is the changing hormonal "climate" of the body a few days before menstruation that is largely responsible for the extreme mood of swings of PMS.

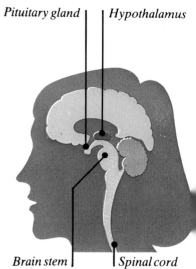

Pituitary gland | Hypothalamus

Brain stem | Spinal cord

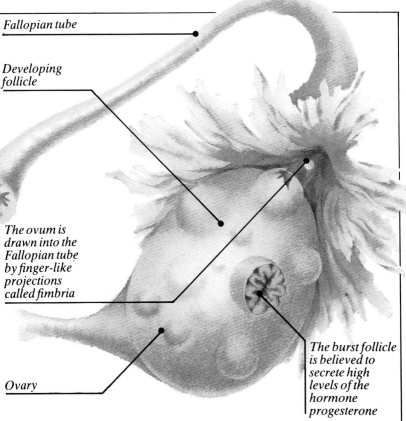

Fallopian tube

Developing follicle

The ovum is drawn into the Fallopian tube by finger-like projections called fimbria

Ovary

The burst follicle is believed to secrete high levels of the hormone progesterone

OVULATION

n the days preceding ovulation about 0 follicles containing the ova begin o grow and develop within the ovary. One or more of these will enlarge still urther and bulge from the ovarian vall, and the ovary will become ngorged with blood, pulling it closer o the uterus.

Eventually one follicle, the tertiary follicle, will grow to half the size of the ovary, and at the moment of ovulation its wall will rupture, releasing the ovum. The ovum in turn bursts through the ovarian wall to begin its journey down the fallopian tube to the uterus.

MENSTRUAL CRAMPS

Many women experience some pain and cramping during menstruation. For most women the cramps subside after the start of the flow. The most common reason for any young woman to take medication today is painful periods.

By keeping a menstrual diary, a woman can predict when she is likely to suffer abdominal discomfort and can take preventative or helpful measures. Evidence shows that a hormone called prostaglandin is responsible not only for initiating labor but also can cause tissue inflammation and muscle spasms during menstruation.

To combat menstrual cramps you might try some of these steps:

● Most women find that relaxation techniques such as deep breathing or meditation are very helpful in relieving the build-up of tension and the cramps that can accompany periods.

● Get extra rest before and during your period.

● A heating pad or hot-water bottle wrapped in a towel and applied to the abdomen may help relieve the pain from cramps.

● Some women find that exercise eases the flow and relieves the constipation and water retention· often experienced during the period.

● High doses of Vitamin B$_6$ help relieve the symptoms for some women.

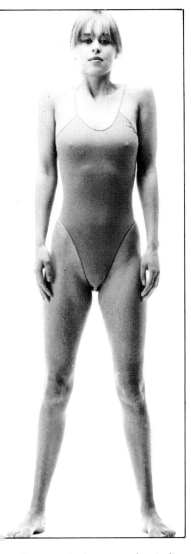

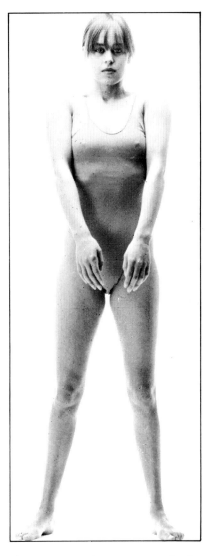

egular exercise *increases the vitality* *the blood circulation and almost* *evitably makes the body feel more* *althy and relaxed. The following* *ercises are particularly helpful in* *hieving this sense of well-being.* *rst, stand with your feet apart, arms* *your side, and breathe in deeply.*

As soon *as your lungs are completely* *full, start to breathe out slowly and* *evenly through the nose. When your* *lungs are empty, raise your shoulders* *and rotate your arms forward across* *the front of your chest, as if you are* *trying to squeeze the last traces of air* *from your lungs. Repeat until you feel* *relaxed.*

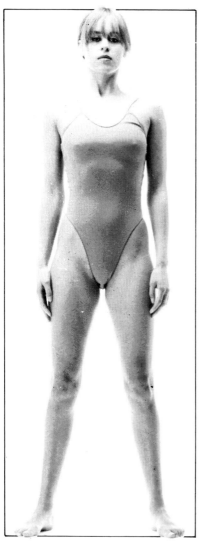

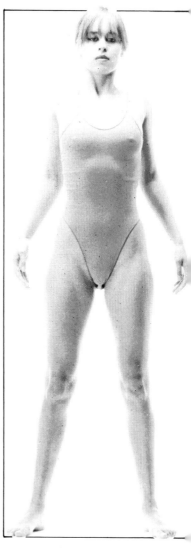

Another helpful *and relaxing breathing exercise also involves a shoulder movement. Stand first with the feet apart and the arms hanging straight down at the side. Breathe in smoothly and evenly.*

When your lungs *feel full, hold your breath and stretch your shoulders back as far as you can. Then bring your shoulders forward again, breathe out steadily and relax. Repea several times.*

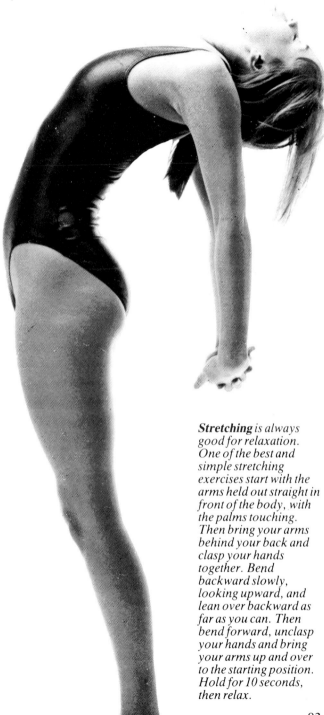

Stretching is always good for relaxation. One of the best and simple stretching exercises start with the arms held out straight in front of the body, with the palms touching. Then bring your arms behind your back and clasp your hands together. Bend backward slowly, looking upward, and lean over backward as far as you can. Then bend forward, unclasp your hands and bring your arms up and over to the starting position. Hold for 10 seconds, then relax.

83

STRESS

Stress is a problem that is becoming increasingly common, give
the strains of life in the highly technological society of today. Man
minor aches and pains, such as tension headaches and backache:
are caused by stress. The reasons it is important to recognize sign
of stress are clear-cut and obvious. If allowed to increased ur
checked, stress can lead not only to aches but to disease. Look fc
signs such as disturbances in your normal eating and sleeping pa:
terns. Some common indications of stress, such as aches in th
muscles and feelings of extreme tiredness, are also early signs c
influenza or other viral infections. Stress reduces your resistance t
disease, so germs can take hold and make you sick.

Stress is rarely the single cause of an illness. More frequently
tends to emphasize existing bodily weaknesses. A minor probler
may hardly be noticed in normal circumstances, but during times c
stress it may grow worse, as part of the general deterioration c
your health. Certain conditions are known to have definite links t
stress. Hypertension (high blood pressure), which may lead t
heart disease, is among these.

The best way to deal with stress is to learn how to cope with you
problems or worries. Try talking to your friends and family fc
support. Sometimes you'll find that your problems are shared b
many people and not just centered on you. Stress can also be r
duced by the enjoyment that comes from a hobby or pastime th:
takes your mind off your troubles.

RELIEVING STRESS

Exercise is a very good way to reduce stress. It relieves the tensio
in your body and helps you relax. One easy, effective exercise is th
stretch. Reach up and out with your arms and stretch toward th
ceiling. Open your mouth and try to yawn. Then stretch out one le
and tighten up the muscles. Bring the leg back and relax it. Repe:
with the other leg.

Another good exercise uses deep breathing to help you rela:
Stand upright with your arms almost touching above your head an
your feet turned slightly outward. Let your arms drop loosel:
exhaling as they cross in front of you. Raise your arms, inhalir
deeply, as you repeat the exercise by bringing them above yo
head.

*Painting a landscape or some other
peaceful scene can bring a real sense
of relaxation.*

Making sensible, constructive choices involves balancing pros and cons, facing reality rather than how you would wish things to be assessing a number of factors from finances to personality and close relationships. It also involves taking risks, having the courage to go with a vision or an ideal rather than being side-tracked by "advice", by comparing yourself to others, by social conventions or stereotypes. All this is a skill, and a difficult one, which must be learnt.

Everyone today talks about stress. But while most people know what it feels like to be "under stress", suffering exhaustion, worry, tension and fear, few know exactly what stress is. The popular image of stress is of some external "thing", like viruses and bacteria, waiting to strike. People think of stress as an inevitable consequence of living in the modern world, just as they assume they will get colds every winter.

But it is wrong to feel that its consequences are inevitable, that it cannot be controlled. We do have control over the stress in our lives and we can learn to manage potentially stressful situations to our advantage, turning a negative response into a positive one by rising to a challenge.

Dr Hans Selye, one of the great pioneers into stress, developed the theory that underlying all illness there is a general body response which is the same regardless of the cause of stress. This is the "fight or flight response", and is governed by the autonomic nervous system.

The autonomic nervous system controls most involuntary body functions: heart beat, regulation of blood pressure, digestive juices, hormonal changes, and so on. There are two sides to the autonomic nervous system which together maintain balance in the body — the sympathetic and the parasympathetic side.

The sympathetic division is concerned with arousal and energy expenditure, and produces what is called the "fight or flight response" because the reaction to a perceived threat is to fight or to run away. This mechanism is stimulated by the pituitary and adrenal glands. Adrenaline and norepinephrine are secreted into the blood stream and the symptoms of arousal follow.

Situations eliciting the stress response can be physical or emotional, real or imagined. Physical exercise also arouses the body but has a positive effect by discharging the energy called upon. Hearing a bump in the night sparks off the stress response, which will continue until you are reassured that nothing is wrong. Once the "danger" has passed, the parasympathetic division brings the body back to a state of stability, calm and rest.

What has happened today, however, is that there are almost constantly threatening situations, from the pressures of work and balancing several roles at once, to the dangers of traffic, city living and

FIGHT OR FLIGHT

Symptoms of stress	Return to normal
● Increased heart rate. ● Faster and harder breathing. ● Perspiration and sweaty palms. ● Increased blood pressure. ● Increased blood sugar level (source of immediate energy). ● Inhibition of gastric juices and diversion of energy away from digestion to the muscles. ● Tension in preparation. ● Increased concentration or attention. ● Emotional changes such as edginess, fear or rage.	● Slowing of heart beat. ● Slowing of breathing with decreased need for oxygen. ● Blood pressure goes down. ● Muscles relax. ● Blood flow moves back from muscles to rest of body and body functions. ● Perspiration stops. ● Concentration relaxes. ● Emotions return to the normal, stable state.

pollution which require our full attention — an exhausting demand. Added to this are the greater threats to humanity which we are all having to live with for the first time, such as the nuclear threat, and ecological and economic breakdown. Many people have to live with an almost continuous state of stress.

The constant tension produced by attempts to deal with prolonged stress has a number of harmful effects on health and well-being. Although people's emotional response to constant and immediate stress varies according to cultural background, upbringing and temperament (some will cry, others maintain a stiff upper lip), the physical consequences of prolonged stress are more universal.

Tension resides not just in the muscles of the limbs and the torso but also in the organs: the lungs (breathing may be rhythmic, rapid or shallow), bladder and kidneys (elimination processes may suffer), the stomach (causing nausea, indigestion, constipation or diarrhea). You may hold the tension in your head and neck as headaches or eve migraines. Other common symptoms are insomnia, late or painfu periods, twitching or heavy eyelids, grinding of the teeth, chroni fatigue, sweaty palms or underarms, bad circulation with clamm hands and feet, rashes, compulsive eating or sudden cravings, con sistent overeating, a dry mouth and a generally, slightly dizzy feelin affecting overall composure.

There are also many common and more severe ailments directl associated with stress — skin disorders such as acne and eczema arthritis, peptic and duodenal ulcers, dandruff, diabetes, asthma an menstrual disorders.

Stress increases vulnerability to viral and bacterial infections too, i that the immune system is greatly impaired. It is affected by increase cortisone levels in the blood stream; fewer white blood cells are pro duced, fewer lymphocytes and less immunoglobulin A (IgA) (all c which fight infections). Stress is also cited as a factor in cancer.

The first step in learning to cope with stress is to get clear in you mind the distinction between an external stressor, and an internal stres response. The external stressor — aggression from your boss, demand from your children, work pressure, accidents — is not automatically cause of stress, it is only a potential source. Much more important i how you perceive that potential stress. It is your perception of it a either a threat, positive challenge or neutral claim on your energy which determines whether you respond with the stress response, th fight-or-flight arousal mechanism. For example, hard physical work o exercise are external stressors but they are viewed positively and ar coped with accordingly. Stress can be a challenge and a spur to achieve ment; it stimulates creativity and makes for variety in life.

These intrinsic drives are a normal part of being human. But what ha happened in the modern workd is that these drives have gone into auto matic and it is they, more than the external stressors that are harmful One reason for this is that stress is addictive. Adrenaline and other hor mones involved in the stress response give the body a "high", and jus like artificial stimulants, this is very addictive, making "normal" lif seem boring.

The second step in coping with stress is to realize that althoug extrinsic stress factors are not necessarily controllable, you can b aware of them and alter your reactions to things that have previousl aroused you. You can also, through relaxation or meditation tech niques, gradually change your inner stressful drives, emotiona volatility, tendency to rush, and so on. Pretending that nothing out ther bothers you is not the answer; it does not make the stress go away. Bu knowing that you can control your responses to stress is an enormou

STRESS FACTORS	
Extrinsic	**Intrinsic**
● Impatience, anger, anxiety and other highly emotional states. ● Lack of assertion skills in threatening situations. ● Feeling guilty about relaxing; restlessness. ● Constant activity. ● Over-identification with work. ● Inability to be satisfied with achievement. ● Doing things constantly in haste. ● Feeling responsible and worrying about things outside your control. ● Need to control. ● Difficulty in listening and in absorbing what is said — preoccupation with your own thoughts.	● Work pressure, deadlines. ● Multiple jobs and roles. ● Bereavement. ● Marriage. ● Birth of a child. ● Financial hardship. ● Unemployment. ● Examinations. ● Having to make decisions quickly. ● Living alone against one's wishes. ● Difficult relationships. ● Conflicts of any sort but particularly between one's needs, desires and social demands. ● The struggle to adapt more quickly than we can to situations.

step towards releasing yourself from the downward spiral of struggle, effort, coping and exhaustion.

The third step is to appreciate the value of slowing down, of rest and inactivity. Far from being wasted time, a slow, thoughtful approach towards one's goals often yields better and more satisfying results. Research shows that much of the pressure of time is, in fact, a subjective feeling rather than a real threat, so think twice about all those deadlines and pressures before you say, "But I can't take things slowly, what about..." Research has also shown that those people who feel that there is never enough time and that they must hurry to get things done, do not actually achieve more than people who work at a more measured pace. The most creative people and those who seem to achieve most have all learnt the value of also taking time out to do nothing, to wander in the park to sit and just think for a while. Often it is the empty space, the silence or the gaps between activity that allow fresh vitality, new insights or changed awareness and perception.

The fourth step in stress management is distancing yourself from potential sources of stress. This does not mean adopting a selfish "I don't care" attitude, but having the ability to look objectively at a situation, and to assess the reality of demands being made. It is easy to work oneself into a panic quite out of proportion to the reality of a situation, or to get so identified with the people or work you are involved with that you lose sight of needs and your abilities.

Ask yourself, "Do I really derive satisfaction from this job or that relationship or is it simply a habit and a drain on my energy'? "Do I really want to meet this challenge or ultimately would it be better for me to steer clear of what is another stress trap for me?"

One solution to stress is to change your living circumstances. For instance, if you have always been a city-dweller, you may decide to move to the country, away from the tensions of city life. Or you may alter your responses to the sources of stress. The first solution, even if it were desirably or possible for most people, is a false one. The very business of living, involves unavoidable stressful situations from births, relationships, illness and death to examinations, board meetings, travel, work deadlines, coping with small children, and so on.

Some fortunate people have such a sanguine temperament that they can emerge unflustered from even the most stressful situations. They can make their daily journey to work pondering inner thoughts, remaining calm and conserving their energy for the day ahead. For many others, the journey itself causes tension and irritation. Blood pressure rises, adrenalin and norepinephrine are secreted into the blood stream, muscles tense, teeth are clenched, heads throb and bodies are keyed up and exhausted before the working day begins.

Although relaxation techniques cannot magically transform you into a calm human being who will remain impervious to stress, if practiced regularly they can help you to cultivate a greater awareness of self, a greater sensitivity to the way your body functions, and to control and quieten the stress responses.

It is important, however, that anyone practicing a relaxation technique should do so regularly, preferably every day, because in this way it becomes absorbed into the pattern of life. You don't have to think about it, or make a conscious effort to fit it in. Otherwise, it would be so easy for this discipline to become simply another source of stress.

The second reason for practicing relaxation techniques regularly is that the effects are cumulative. Like any retraining of the body, and particularly one that involves the weaning of the body away from an addiction (whether cigarettes, alcohol or stress), it takes time.

Also, you should practice relaxation techniques without expectations. Make this one area of your life which is not goal-oriented, where you do not have to achieve anything, compete with anyone or please anyone but yourself. This is your time, your space, in which to get to know yourself and your inner center. The techniques help you to release consciously your whole body, and involve getting to know where and how to hold tension and how to release that tension. They focus in turn on different parts of the body — limbs, stomach, neck, head — allowing you to relax each until your whole body is still, relaxed and peaceful. This state is quite different from that of "flopping". You feel very alert and aware, without being tense.

Gradually you can incorporate what you learn into your daily life even when not consciously practicing the technique. You become tuned to recognizing points and moments of tension and are able to release and let go of these causes of stress without going through the full relaxation process.

Reading your favorite author in comfort at home is a very effective way of relaxing.

Stretch your arms up and outward as far as you can. Yawn if you want to. Alternately stretch and contract the muscles of one leg then the other.

Hold your arms out in front of your chest, then suddenly let both drop and swing down past your hips and out behind. Repeat several times.

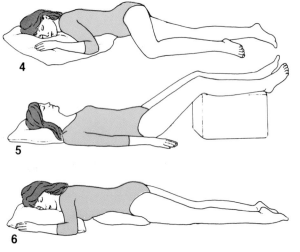

Some positions for lying down are more relaxing than others. Try lying face down with one leg slightly bent (top), to help relax abdominal muscles.
Lie on your back with your feet raised (middle), to help the circulation. Lie face down with a pillow beneath your abdomen (bottom), to ease back tension.

3 _Hold your arms high above your head, then let them drop loosely, swinging outward and across the front of your body. Repeat rhythmically._

RELAXING NATURALLY

Exercise has long been recognized as a useful way of reducing stress. It may help by stretching muscles that have tightened up during the day or just by allowing you to work off excess physical energy.

Relaxing naturally after work at home is one of the best times to loosen up. Relax for just a few minutes each day — while planning your evening perhaps — by following a gentle exercise routine and feel some of the tension drain out of the body.

If fitness exercises are not your favorite relaxation technique, relax by listening to music, reading a good book, playing a game of chess or going for a walk.

INDEX

Page numbers in *italic* refer to the illustrations and captions